DANGEROUS COAST:
Pictured Rocks Shipwrecks

by Frederick Stonehouse

and

Daniel R. Fountain

DANGEROUS COAST:
Pictured Rocks Shipwrecks

by Frederick Stonehouse
and
Daniel R. Fountain

Copyright 1997
by Avery Color Studios

Library of Congress Card # 97-071228
ISBN # 0-932212-93-X
First Edition April 1997

Published
by Avery Color Studios
Marquette, Michigan 49855

TABLE OF CONTENTS

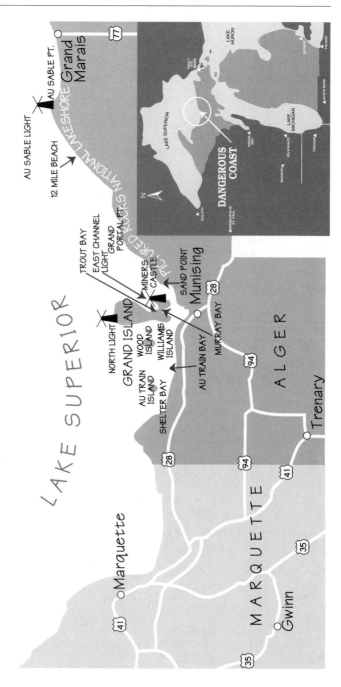

Chapter One

EARLY HISTORY

Lake Superior played the pivotal role in the development of the entire Upper Great Lakes region. Every major activity - fur trading, lumbering and mining, used the lake as the highway to success. The Pictured Rocks, comprising some of the most treacherous coastline on the lake, were central to much of this navigation, while Grand Island and its natural harbor offered the only shelter from the lake's fury for miles around. Thus it is not surprising that the area was the scene of numerous shipwrecks through the years.

The first commercial use of the lake was in the late 1600's by the early French voyageurs when they sought the region's rich furs. Initially the voyageurs used frail birch bark canoes until an increase in trade required the use of larger bateaux and later small schooners. Year after year, this hardy breed of intrepid men ventured north and west from the Soo, their destinations the scattered trading posts along the Superior shore. Principal posts were at La Pointe, Wisconsin, and Grand Portage, Minnesota. Minor posts were in the Pictured Rocks area at Grand Marais and Grand Island.

The first vessel constructed on Lake Superior was built in 1735 at Point Aux Pins, north of the Soo, for Louis Denis, Sieur de La Ronde. Only 25 tons burden, she was rigged with two sails. La Ronde used her extensively in the Apostle Islands area and in various copper mining and fur trading activities. The vessel made frequent trips from the

A section of hull on the lonely shore, a stark reminder of a shipwreck long ago.   FREDERICK STONEHOUSE

Apostles to the Soo and it is likely she often passed, stopped or sheltered in the Grand Island or Grand Marais areas.

Point Aux Pins also saw two other vessels built, a 40-ton sloop launched some time after 1763 and another sloop built in 1771. In 1785 another unnamed schooner was hauled over the St. Marys rapids. The North West Company built four schooners at Fort William between 1809 - 1821 and in 1817 dragged the schooner EXMOUTH around the Soo. The Lake Superior fleet grew steadily but slowly. The eventual disposition of these vessels is unknown.

In 1763 the French lost the Lake Superior region to the English. Now it was the English traders who roamed the wild lake and reaped the rich harvest of fur.

Vessel traffic on the lake was light at best. Before the War of 1812, there were only a few small vessels above the St. Marys rapids. One was the 40-ton sloop FUR TRADER, which was later wrecked in an attempt to "shoot" the rapids while running down to the lower lakes. With the 1816 loss of the INVINCIBLE on Whitefish Point and the

1828 departure of the RECOVERY for the lower lakes, there were no vessels left on the lake larger than a Mackinaw boat. This depressed state of navigation remained for seven years.

The year 1835 saw the launching of one of the most famous vessels in Lake Superior history, the schooner JOHN JACOB ASTOR, named for the owner of the powerful American Fur Company. Owned by the company, the 78-foot, 112-ton vessel was built of white oak from the Black River area of Ohio. The ASTOR, under the command of either of the legendary Stannard brothers, Benjamin or Charles, was used to carry passengers and freight between the scattered Lake Superior posts of the Astors' fur trading empire. In 1844 she was lost in a gale at Copper Harbor.

After the ASTOR, the number of vessels on Lake Superior began to grow steadily. In 1837 another American Fur Company vessel, the MADELINE, was on the lake and engaged in fishing activities. The following year the 73-ton WILLIAM BREWSTER, 60-ton ALGON-QUIN and 40-ton SISKAWIT were all hauled past the St. Marys rapids into Lake Superior and were actively engaged in either trading or fishing.

The lake vessel count increased dramatically in 1845, with ten new vessels being brought over the rapids. Unique among the fleet was the propeller INDEPENDENCE, the first steamer on the lake. This historic craft was lost in 1853 when her boilers exploded in the St. Marys River. Other new vessels included the SWALLOW, CHIPPEWA, FLORENCE, UNCLE TOM, OCEAN, FUR TRADER (different from the earlier vessel), WHITE FISH, NAPOLEON, and MERCHANT. Some of the early steamers were incredibly inefficient. For example in 1847 the sidewheeler JULIA PALMER once took 16 days to run the 200 miles from Copper Harbor to the Soo. Fuel grew so short, they burned everything aboard, including furniture and cargo!

The sudden increase in shipping was caused by the twin discoveries of the vast iron deposits of the Marquette Range and of copper on the Keweenaw Peninsula in 1844. Eagerly the new ships carried the men and supplies that would pioneer the new mines and open the riches to development. Quickly the small settlements at Eagle Harbor, Eagle River, Marquette, L'Anse and Ontonagon assumed major importance as ports for the expanding mining industry. From 1850-1875 the Keweenaw mines provided more than 75 per cent of all the copper mined in the U.S.

With the opening of the St. Marys Fall Ship Canal (Soo Locks) in 1855, lake commerce truly burgeoned. Now ships could sail directly between Lake Superior and Lake Huron. Previously, cargos had to be transshipped overland around the St. Marys rapids, an expensive and time consuming proposition. If a vessel was to move from lake to lake, it was hauled out of the water and teams of oxen literally pulled it past the mile-long cataracts on large rollers. Over the years new, bigger locks were built as vessel traffic and the size of the ships increased. Today 1,000-foot freighters navigate the lakes.

Since the Soo Locks provided the means for cheap transportation of ore from the mines to the lower lakes mills, the iron mines stepped into high gear. Soon a veritable river of the red ore was flowing from the Ishpeming and Negaunee shafts to the docks at Marquette and on down the lakes to the mills. Vessel traffic to the iron port quickly increased from one or two a week to that number in a day. At first the ore was laboriously loaded into the schooners by the basketful. Later, when larger and stronger vessels were used, it was loaded directly into the holds by chutes from the new "pocket" docks.

The ready availability of large amounts of ore, charcoal made from local hardwoods, and nearby deposits of limestone led many area businessmen to the conclusion that a major iron making industry could be established in the Lake Superior region. Between 1848 and 1922, 33 different iron forges and furnaces operated in the Upper Peninsula of Michigan. The furnaces produced iron blooms or "pigs" that would be shipped to manufacturing centers in Chicago, Milwaukee or Detroit. Old sailors recalled that by night, ships approaching Marquette harbor could see the deep red glow of the city's forges brightening the dark sky.

Two iron furnaces were located in the Munising area. Near the present site of Christmas, then known as Onota, the Bay Furnace operated between 1870 and 1877. Today the site is a Forest Service campground. To facilitate loading and unloading, a 1,400-foot dock stretched out into deep water. Part of the furnace is still standing and is a local tourist attraction. The second furnace, the Schoolcraft or Munising Furnace, was on the shore of the east channel, now within the boundaries of the Pictured Rocks National Lakeshore. It operated from 1868 to 1877, producing 15-20 tons of pig iron daily. Today little of the furnace is visible. Both furnaces relied on local shipping to bring in the supplies of raw ore and limestone, as well as to carry out the cast iron pigs. The remains of pier structures can be found near each of the furnace sites. The entire iron industry failed due to simple economics. It proved far cheaper to transport large cargos of ore to the lower lakes and make iron there, than to make it locally. Also, a shift from charcoal iron to a coke-based variety required the transport of large amounts of coke north to the Superior furnaces, an uneconomical proposition. Iron ore was a nearly indestructible cargo; rain, heat, and cold had no effect on it. By contrast, coke was far more sensitive and did not travel as well.

During the period following the 1855 opening of the Soo Canal, schooners were the predominant means of lake transportation, although the numbers of huffing, puffing, smoke belching steamboats were growing steadily. Abraham Williams, the earliest Grand Island pioneer, operated a fueling station for wood burning steamers for many years. Until coal supplanted wood as a fuel for steamers, the island was a popular stopping point to replenish cordwood stocks. An early steamer had to stop for wood every eight to ten hours.

The high point for sail on the Great Lakes was 1868, when there were 1,856 vessels totaling some 294,000 tons. In 1873 the number had decreased to 1,663 vessels, but the replacement of older, smaller craft with newer, larger ones raised the tonnage total to 298,000! In comparison, during the same year there were 2,642 hulls of all types on the lakes, totaling 521,000 tons. At the time, sail had 63 percent of the hulls and 57 percent of the tonnage! A fast, well-built schooner was a good investment. With good management and a little luck, she could pay for herself in a mere two years!

The decline of the graceful sailing vessel was rapid. By 1880 there were only 1400 left on the lakes and by 1900 only 800! Many of those left had been converted to humble schooner-barges. Sail craft declined for numerous reasons. They depended on favorable winds and were difficult to maneuver in narrow and winding channels or rivers. Usually tugs were needed to pull them through these difficult stretches as well as in and out of harbors, all of which added to operating expense. As the lake traffic increased, the schooner cargo holds proved too small to be efficient.

Long since supplanted by the steamers in the passenger and general freight trade, the sailing vessels for a time found work hauling bulk cargos of iron ore, stone, coal and lumber. Gradually, however, these cargos also became uneconomical. Many of the schooners were relegated to the roles of schooner-barges. These vessels were often nothing more than normal schooners with their topmasts removed and all sails and hamper removed except for the mainsails, fore and aft. Since a small crew of four or five was carried, a schooner-barge could make some sail in an emergency, perhaps just enough to hold her head to the sea or haul off a rock coast if her tow line parted. "Strings" of up to six schooner-barges were towed behind a steamer or tug. This proved to be a very efficient arrangement, except for the large number of parted tow lines which added constantly to the toll of wrecks.

The change from sail to steam also spelled the end to an era of another kind, the time when a captain could own or be a part owner of his vessel and manage her affairs. The new steamers were too large an investment for a mere seaman. Instead large shipping concerns owned and managed the vessels. The captain was reduced to nothing more than a employee. No longer was he truly the master of his ship.

Along with the change of ownership came a change in names. Imaginative and graceful names like ANTELOPE, ISLE ROYALE, LADY ELGIN, MOONLIGHT and SUNBEAM were gone. In their place the newer steamers carried the names of captains of industry. The JOHN B. TREVOR, CHESTER A. CONGDON, HENRY B. SMITH, and JOHN B. COWLE are prime examples. This practice continues to the present day with the ships of the inland seas often named for their corporate sponsors.

New innovations were constantly occurring that revolutionized Great Lakes shipping. In 1869, the first bulk freighter, the 211-foot steamer R.J. HACKETT, was launched at Cleveland. With a capacity of 1,200 tons she was the prototype for an entire class of vessels.

In 1882 the first iron hulled steamer, the 287-foot ONOKO, was built. Although she was lost in 1915 on Lake Superior, it wasn't due to her iron construction but rather as the result of storm stress. 1886 saw the launching of the first steel steamer, the 310-foot SPOKANE. In a short 17 years the quantum leap from wooden schooner to steel bulk freighter had been made. Technology marched on. The nation's growing need for Lake Superior iron ore for the lower lake steel mills demanded still more efficient vessels. And the ship builders complied with longer, wider and deeper hulls.

In 1906, a mere eighteen years after the SPOKANE set the standard for new vessels, thirty-four freighters with a capacity to 12,000 tons and lengths to 550 feet were launched. The modern bulk freighters grew so rapidly that their capacity was nearly double those of only three years earlier. Along with the increase in size, cargo handling efficiency was also improved. In the 1870's it took a week to unload 1,000 tons of ore with picks, shovels, wheel barrows and human backs. Later monstrous mechanical Hulett unloaders did the job in mere hours.

As a result of vessel size and subsequent economy, shipping rates also fell. In 1867 the rate for ore delivered from Marquette to Cleveland was $4.25 a ton. Five years later it was $2.50, and in 1897 only $.50 per ton.

The cost to build new boats also fell as shipyards grew more efficient, from roughly $7.00 a ton for a 2,500-ton vessel in 1885, to $5.00 a ton for a 5,000-ton vessel in 1898.

Traffic on Lake Superior grew as dramatically as vessel size. In 1889 only 25 percent of Great Lakes commerce was on Lake Superior. In 1906 she carried nearly half! More traffic in tonnage passed through the Soo Canal than the world famous Suez Canal.

In 1865 Michigan's Upper Peninsula mines were a significant producer of America's iron ore. By 1890 the Michigan mines were producing 45 percent of all the U.S. iron ore. When the great Minnesota mines also stepped into high gear at the turn of the century, the Lake Superior iron district was supplying the vast majority of America's needs. Ship after ship heavily loaded with cargos of rich iron ore steamed down from Superior to the great steel mills of Cleveland, Buffalo and Chicago. Despite competition from cheaply mined imported ore, in 1995 Lake Superior mines supplied over 78 percent of the United States steel industry's requirements for iron ore.

The number of shipwrecks increased in direct proportion to the amount of traffic on the lake. In the wake of every major storm, area newspapers were filled with reports of numerous wrecked and missing vessels. The worst year for Superior was 1905, when 38 major wrecks were recorded. To date there have been approximately 550 major losses on Lake Superior. In the twenty year period between 1878 and 1898, nearly 6,000 vessels were wrecked on the Great Lakes. An estimated 1,090 were total losses. By contrast, Lake Superior losses during the same period totaled approximately 137, with 80 being total losses. Since overall vessel traffic was lighter on Superior, the number of losses was less. But if a vessel was wrecked on the big lake, the likelihood of the loss being total was much greater.

Traditionally, the navigation season on Lake Superior ran from the end of April to the middle of December. During the harsh winter the Soo Locks would close, effectively sealing off Lake Superior. As an examination of the vessel loss section will show, by far the most dangerous time for vessels was during the early spring and late fall. It was then that the lake could be expected to lash out with storms of incredible fury. Of the two periods, though, it was the fall that was the most vicious. Vessel after vessel succumbed to the "gales of November."

The Michigan shoreline of Lake Superior from Au Sable Point west to Au Train was an area of particular danger. The reasons are many and interrelated such that the total danger equals more than the sum of the individual parts. The long coastline is irregular and presents a variety of features: high sand mountains at Grand Sable Dunes, towering rock cliffs of the Pictured Rocks, the long projection of Grand Island and the twisting, sweeping shore near Au Train. All are natural death traps for unwary vessels. The prevailing north winds (which have an alarming propensity for turning into roaring north gales) could easily drive a vessel into destruction on any of the dangerous coastal features. Au Sable Reef, stretching north from Au Sable Point, is a hazard to be avoided at all costs. The entire coastline, but especially Au Sable Point, is notorious for thick fogs. Together all of these features spelled trouble for numerous vessels and total destruction for many others. Since a common navigational method was to "coast" along the shore, the special dangers described became obvious.

The appalling loss of life due to shipwreck on the Atlantic coast as well as on the Great Lakes eventually forced the government to construct lighthouses and other aids to navigation and later to establish life-saving stations in areas of highest danger. The first such stations were on the Atlantic coast and were manned strictly by volunteers, although the government did provide the equipment. After a series of disastrous shipwrecks it became evident that the system of volunteer stations would not work and a professional U.S. Life-Saving Service was formed under the auspices of the Treasury Department.

The first life-saving stations on Lake Superior were established in 1877 at Vermilion Point, Big Two-Hearted River, Crisp's Point, and Muskallonge Lake. These early stations were thinly spread over the dangerous strip of shore known as the "shipwreck coast" running from the Whitefish Point west to Grand Marais. Additional life-saving stations were later built at Portage Ship Canal in 1885, Marquette in 1891, Duluth in 1896, Grand Marais, Michigan in 1901, and Eagle Harbor in 1912. Eventually Coast Guard lifeboat stations were also opened at Grand Marais, Minnesota, Ashland-Bayfield, Wisconsin, Whitefish Point and Munising, Michigan.

By 1893 there were a total of forty-seven life-saving stations on the Great Lakes. Each was manned by a keeper and usually a minimum of eight surfmen, numbered one through eight based on ability and experience. In the absence of the keeper, the number one surfman assumed charge. Although the crews were paid, they were only paid during the season. When the stations shut down in the winter, the men were forced to find other employment.

Quickly the rugged men of the Life-Saving Service built an incredible reputation for ability and courage. Time and time again these men performed the impossible, challenging monstrous seas and screaming winds to accomplish desperate rescues. Referred to as "storm warriors" in contemporary news accounts, their reputation was untarnished. They were the heroes of the public. In between the moments of incredible bravery, though, were long periods of monotonous inactivity and drill. Again and again, under the critical eyes of the keeper, the crew rehearsed every skill necessary to their trade. When the time for action came, they were ready.

In a 1915 government-inspired reorganization, the Life-Saving Service was combined with the Revenue Marine to form the present United States Coast Guard, thus ending a glorious chapter in American history. Although the traditions of the old Life-Saving Service continued for a short period in the fledgling Coast Guard, the eventual retirement of the original Life-Savers, increasing mechanization and a larger burden of official red tape slowly ended the legendary tradition of the "storm warriors." They now live only in history.

The Grand Marais Life-Saving Station, opened in 1901, was built on a site donated by the Grand Marais Lumber Company. The rescue exploits performed by the Grand Marais crew were among the most spectacular in the Great Lakes. The Coast Guard station that replaced it is long gone and the facility is now a Pictured Rocks National Lakeshore maritime museum. The local Coast Guard Auxiliary however, continues to perform a vital role in maritime safety and carries on the rich traditions of the old crews.

In the calm bays of Grand Marais, Munising and Grand Island early Indians found fine camping grounds well sheltered from the north gales. The Indians who inhabited the area were the Ojibway or Chippewa. They existed primarily on hunting and fishing with a little

East Channel and the Pictured Rocks.　　　DANIEL R. FOUNTAIN

agriculture. The Pictured Rocks area however, was never a major center of Indian activities. The rugged and inhospitable coast prevented easy access by water and a lack of ready food sources inland precluded permanent settlement.

The Pictured Rocks did have some minor religious significance to the Indians. As was common in aboriginal cultures, they attached religious significance to inanimate objects. Thus the rocks and caves of the cliffs were personified as devils, ghosts, etc. Certainly many of the stories grew as the newly arriving Europeans embellished the original Indian legends. Many of these tales are retold in Beatrice Castle's book *Grand Island Story.*

It isn't certain who the first Europeans to see the Pictured Rocks were but it could have been the French explorers Etienne Brule and a man known to history only as Grenoble. Some time around 1622 the intrepid pair reached a previously unknown lake above Huron, (Lake Superior) but what they saw was ill-recorded. The first Europeans definitely known to have explored the Pictured Rocks area were the legendary French voyageur Pierre Esprit Radisson with his brother-in-law Medard Chouart, Sieur des Groseilliers in 1659. The pair were searching for new sources of fur, an effort that would reap tremendous reward. Strangely, the French would reject the discovery of the seemingly limitless bounty of Superior, leading Radisson to join the British and help to found the famous Hudson's Bay Company. It's not unlikely that the pair of intrepid travellers camped somewhere along the coast between Grand Marais and Au Train. The great fleets of voyageurs that later followed certainly did. By 1668 the French were well familiar with Superior's south shore and considered all of it part of New France. With the Peace of Paris in 1763 the area was ceded to the British, and in 1783 the region became part of the fledgling United States.

Other famous men also coasted the area. In 1660 Jesuit priest Rene Menard passed with Jesuit Claude Allouez following in 1664. Jacques Marquette, another old Jesuit, passed in 1669 en route to his La Pointe mission.

Grand Island was known to the native Chippewa as Kitchi Miniss, meaning "great island." The island's Murray Bay is named for John Murray, one of the earliest settlers. The story goes that he was born in Ireland in the early 1800's and educated for the priesthood. Unfortunately, he fell in love with a girl who was evidently betrothed to his cousin. The two men fought a bloody duel over the Irish lass resulting in the death of his cousin and Murray running off to America. After working as a clerk and accountant in New York, he migrated west, eventually reaching Grand Island. There he built a small house on the point of today's Murray Bay and made use of his education by working as a teacher for the children of Grand Island pioneer Abraham Williams and later his grandchildren. By all accounts he was an excellent teacher. Perhaps morose over love long lost, Murray became addicted to drink and as he aged, gradually evolved into a near hermit, staying close to his small home. It was said he often spoke to imaginary visitors as well as unidentified "spirits." He died in 1884.

The village of Onota, established in 1869, was the original major settlement in the Grand Island area. It was located approximately six miles west of the present town of Munising and was owned by the Bay Furnace Company, which built two blast furnaces there, as well as 80 houses and a long dock into the bay. In 1871 Onota became the first county seat of Schoolcraft County, the present Alger County not being formed until 1885. The village was completely destroyed by fire in 1877 and was never rebuilt. In 1940 the village of Christmas was started near the old Onota site. The name was selected to help promote a local toy factory, which was also later destroyed by fire.

West of Onota, the mouth of the Au Train River was a landmark for the local Indians, being the northern end of a portage trail between Lake Michigan and Lake Superior. The village of Au Train was founded in 1881 when the Detroit, Mackinac and Marquette Railroad was being built through the area on its way east. In 1885, when Alger County was formed out of a portion of the earlier Schoolcraft County, the village was chosen as the county seat, an honor soon usurped by the growing village of Munising. In 1887 Au Train had a population of 300 souls.

Grand Marais was named by early French explorers who passed through and occasionally camped along its sheltering bay. The original name was Grand Mare, meaning "great pond." This was later transcribed as Grand Marais, a similar pronunciation meaning "great marsh." The harbor was a welcome refuge for later explorers, missionaries, traders and tourists travelling Superior's south shore. The 1860's saw the first permanent settlement at Grand Marais with the establishment of commercial fishing and lumbering. By the turn of the century the village was a boom town, due primarily to the local sawmills. During its heyday approximately 400 vessels arrived annually. By 1910 the lumber was gone and the town fell into deep decline.

The original settlement at Munising was in the 1850's in the area now known as East Munising. The present site was developed in the 1890's. The town's name comes from the Chippewa name Kitchi Minissing, meaning "place of the great island." With the exception of the small charcoal iron industry, Munising was primarily a lumber town. The first mills were built near the Anna River in 1896. Included was a 350-foot tramway into the bay with a 75-foot long dock running parallel to the shore. Between 1880-1910 Munising flourished as a

Grand Portal around 1850.   DANIEL R. FOUNTAIN

lumber and commercial fishing town, but afterwards declined in importance other than as a harbor of refuge. As a port it never ranked with the major ones on the lake. As is evident in the shipwreck listing however, many vessels sought shelter from storms behind Grand Island or in Munising Harbor. This tradition still continues.

On January 11, 1980 the 730-foot, 21,500-ton Canadian ore carrier ALGOBAY departed Marquette with a cargo of iron ore pellets bound for the Canadian Soo. In the open lake she was pounded by high waves and lashed by 55 mile an hour northwest winds, causing her captain, Alexander Nazar, to seek protection in Munising's South Bay. Being unfamiliar with the channel, he first brought the vessel into shelter behind Grand Island, north of Trout Bay, on the east side of the Island. It was there that Joe Brey, a Munising commercial fisherman, sighted the vessel at 5 p.m. Friday and inquired by radio if all was well. The Captain replied that as long as the wind was from the west, he thought he would be all right. When Brey radioed the ALGOBAY again at 3 a.m. Saturday, the Captain said he was now worried since the swells were running at 15 feet and the wind had shifted more northerly.

He was concerned the vessel could be forced aground. When Brey offered to guide the big vessel to safety in the bay, the ALGOBAY's master agreed. At daybreak Joe with his father Henry Brey and Gordon Snyder used his small fishing boat to guide the ALGOBAY into the harbor where she safely weathered the storm. After the weather moderated on Sunday, she departed to continue her trip to the Soo.

And so the long tradition of sheltering at Grand island continues. Three hundred years ago it was a hardy French voyageur with his frail birch bark canoe pulled safely ashore; today it is a modern ore carrier. Regardless of the vast difference in technology, their need was the same!

There is another important facet to the ALGOBAY incident, namely that it very effectively illustrates the generous and efficient services rendered to those in need by the lakes commercial fishermen. When the men went out into the wild lake to guide the ALGOBAY to safety, there was no thought of reward, only that a vessel was in trouble and needed help. Without the assistance given by the commercial fishermen, the large ALGOBAY could have been in serious trouble and the consequences fatal. Helping others has long been a tradition of the commercial fishermen.

Chapel Rock and the Chapel River.　　　　　　　Daniel R. Fountain

It had been a saying of the old Life-Saving Service (and later the early Coast Guard) that when a vessel was in trouble, no matter how wild the lake, regulations said you had to go out. Nothing, however was said about having to coming back! The commercial fishermen didn't have any dramatic sayings, nor did they share in the public praise given to the colorful "heroes of the surf." But they did go out, regardless of the weather; the lake was their livelihood, nets needed to be set and lifted, the weather was only one more variable. They knew the lake and its many moods as well as the hunter the forest, or the farmer his fields!

The commercial fishermen's rescue work was very important, especially in an area like Munising, too far from the life-saving stations at Grand Marais and Marquette to be able to rely on their services. The short-lived Munising Coast Guard Station was of little help. Although it isn't always documented in the following shipwreck accounts, in many instances it was the fishermen who actually rescued the helpless crews.

As it was in the past, so it still is now. Munising should be glad she still has an active commercial fishing fleet.

The Pictured Rocks comprise a series of sandstone cliffs extending nearly 15 miles northeast from Grand Island Harbor. The Indians called the area Ishpabecca, meaning "high rocks." Early English-speaking explorers named the cliffs the Pictured Rocks for the multitude of colors and patterns on their facades. The sandstone of the cliffs was laid down at the bottom of a shallow sea, sometimes referred to as the Munising Sea, which covered the area some 500 million years ago during the Late Cambrian Period. Over the millennia, Lake Superior has carved the cliffs into fantastic columns, spires, caves and bays. The colors in the cliffs come from minerals such as iron and copper which have leached out of the sandstone layers and become oxidized when they were exposed to the air.

The need to preserve the unique natural beauty of the Pictured Rocks has been recognized for years. The National Park Service in 1958 singled out the area as one of five shoreline areas of national significance on the Great Lakes. In 1966 Congress passed Public Law 89-668, which authorized the formation of the Pictured Rocks National Lakeshore. The Park Service set about acquiring the entire lakeshore from Munising to Grand Marais, obtaining the required property from its government, corporate, and private owners.

The Pictured Rocks National Lakeshore encompasses about 38 miles of coastline and is three miles wide at its widest point. Starting just northeast of Munising, it includes Sand Point, with the Lakeshore headquarters in the old Munising Coast Guard Station. Beyond Sand Point, the Pictured Rocks begin to rise along the shoreline, climbing to where Miners Castle's sandstone buttresses stand 90 feet above the lake. Miners Castle and the adjacent Miners River take their name from the miners of the 1769-1773 Alexander Henry expeditions who camped here and attempted to find mineral riches in the Pictured Rocks. East of the point, the white sand of Miners Beach stretches nearly a mile before the colorful sandstone cliffs again dominate the shoreline. Here the sheer cliffs rise more than 150 feet above the lake's surface for over five miles, giving way briefly to a rocky beach near the mouth of Mosquito River, only to rise again to Grand Portal Point. The natural arch through the point is only a small remnant of the original Grand Portal, an enormous sea cave that once penetrated the west side of the point. The vast domed cave, known to the voyageurs as La Portail, was some 400 feet wide, 180 feet deep, and over 150 feet high. It collapsed years ago, leaving only its outline on the cliff face. Past Grand Portal Point, the cliffs are again interrupted by a small sand beach and the mouth of Chapel River at Chapel Rock. A mile and a half east of the Chapel, Spray Falls marks the site of the 1856 shipwreck of the SUPERIOR. From here on the rock cliffs slowly decline until they meet the sandy shore of Twelvemile Beach. At the eastern end of the beach stands Au Sable Point with its lighthouse, east of which rise the 300-foot high Grand Sable Dunes which stretch to the end of the National Lakeshore at Grand Marais.

Recognizing the historical value of shipwrecks and their vulnerability to salvagers and souvenir hunters, the Michigan Legislature in

1980 enacted Public Act 184 which authorized the formation of under-water preserves to protect such cultural resources on state-owned bottomlands. A citizens' committee in Alger County proposed a preserve for the Munising area and on June 24, 1981, the Alger Underwater Preserve became the first member of the Michigan bottomland preserve system. The Alger preserve extends from Au Train Point to Au Sable Point, including Grand Island, and out to a depth of 150 feet. Within the preserve, it is illegal to remove or disturb any artifacts without a permit jointly issued by the Secretary of State and the Department of Natural Resources; such permits are only issued for historical or scientific purposes. Violators are subject to a prison term of up to two years and a $5000 fine. Many of the popular shipwrecks in the Alger Underwater Preserve are marked with white and blue mooring buoys maintained by volunteers from the Alger Underwater Preserve Committee in an effort to minimize damage to the wrecks from vessels' anchors. Hopefully, these protective measures will help to ensure that these sunken time capsules will be preserved for generations to come.

REFERENCES:

Arthur T. Adams, *The Exploration of Pierre Esprit Radisson,* from the Original Manuscript in the Bodleian Library and British Museum (Minneapolis, Minnesota: Ross and Haines, 1961).

James Davie Butler, *"Early Shipping on Lake Superior,"* Proceedings of State Historical Society of Wisconsin (1894), p. 86.

James L. Carter, *"Au Sable Light, Sentinel of the Great Sands,"* Inland Seas, Volume 33 (Summer, 1977), p. 100.

Cliff's News (Cleveland: The Cleveland Cliffs Iron Co., Third Quarter, 1979).

John A. Dorr, Jr. and Donald F. Eschman, *Geology of Michigan* (Ann Arbor, Michigan: The University of Michigan Press, 1970)

"First Trip by Steam to Lake Superior," *Michigan Pioneer and Historical Collections, Volume IV* (1881), pp. 67-69.

Walter Havighurst, *Men and Iron* (New York: World Publishing, 1958), p. 88

Wilbert B. Hinsdale, *Distribution of Aboriginal Population of Michigan, Occasional Contributions from the Museums of Anthropology of the University of Michigan,* Number 2 (Ann Arbor, Michigan: University Museums, 1932).

Charles K. Hyde, PhD, Director, *The Upper Peninsula of Michigan, An Inventory of Historic Engineering and Industrial Sites.* (Washington, D.C.: U.S. Government Printing Office, 1978), p. 140.

Louise Phelps Kellogg, *The French Regime in Wisconsin and the Northwest.* (New York: Cooper Square Publishing Co., 1968), pp. 59-60, 109, 352-355.

Kenneth D. LaFayette, *Flaming Brands* (Marquette, Michigan: Northern Michigan University Press, 1977), p. 49.

Light List, Volume IV, Great Lakes (Washington, D.C.: U.S. Government Printing Office, 1979).

J.B. Mansfield, *History of the Great Lakes, Volume 1* (Chicago: J.H. Beers, 1899), pp. 194-197.

Mining Journal (Marquette), July 29, 1871, January 17, 1980.

Dennis L. Noble and T. Michael O'Brien, *Sentinels of the Rocks* (Marquette, Michigan: Northern Michigan University Press, 1979), p. 27.

Grace Lee Nute, *Lake Superior* (New York: Bobbs Merrill, 1944), pp. 134-137.

Bernard Peters, *Lake Superior Place Names: From Bawating to the Montreal* (Marquette, Michigan: Northern Michigan University Press, 1996), pp. 44-58

Charles Symon, Editor, *Alger County: A Centennial History* (Munising, Michigan: Bayshore Press, 1985)

Julius F. Wolff, Jr., *"One Hundred Years of Rescues: The Coast Guard on Lake Superior,"* Inland Seas, Volume 31 (Winter, 1975), p. 256.

CHAPTER TWO

THE TOTAL LOSSES

MERCHANT
June 13, 1847

Research has indicated that the first major American vessel to join Superior's fleet of the "Went Missing" was the small 74-ton topsail schooner MERCHANT. On June 12, 1847 the schooner left Sault Ste. Marie, Michigan with a heavy cargo of mining supplies and foodstuffs consigned to the Keweenaw copper mines, seven passengers, and a crew of seven. Most of the crew were Canadians, while the cook was a free black man from Detroit.

Sources do not all agree regarding the number of crew and passengers. One source states she carried fifteen soldiers bound for Fort Wilkins at Copper Harbor on Keweenaw Point as well as fifteen men employed by the National Mining Company. The fourteen man figure however, is probably the most reliable.

Regardless of the crew size, the men were hardly overpaid, at least by today's inflated standards. Average wages ran about one dollar a day!

Captain Robert Moore, her regular master, was not in command since he had broken his leg the previous day while coming ashore. Instead, Captain Robert Brown of the schooner SWALLOW had agreed to take the trip in his place.

The small schooner MERCHANT, lost somewhere near Grand Island.
C. PATRICK LABADIE

Like many of his contemporaries, Captain Brown appears to have believed in many of the old lake superstitions. On one occasion after hearing that Reverend John Pitezel, a famous Methodist missionary, had experienced an especially difficult storm-tossed trip on the brig JOHN JACOB ASTOR, Brown claimed the troubles were the direct result of having a boat full of women and preachers. He said he "never knew it to fail, with women and preachers aboard, sailors were sure to have storms!" Pitezel couldn't understand why the "fair sex" would "influence the spirit of storms" against the sailors, unless it was in repayment for the many "long and painful neglects they have suffered from those who have followed the sea."

The MERCHANT left the Soo with an official destination of the Keweenaw area. Since three of the passengers were Vermont lumbermen under contract to work at the L'Anse mills, the assumption can be made that a stop there was also planned. On the night of June 13, a furious gale swept across Lake Superior, and presumably during this storm the MERCHANT sank. As news of the whereabouts of the schooner failed to reach the Soo, fears for the safety of the MERCHANT mounted. After three weeks, the conclusion was reluctantly drawn that the vessel was lost with all hands. To help determine her fate, Captain Moore searched the lake aboard another schooner but failed to find a trace of the missing MERCHANT.

The only item of identifiable wreckage recovered from the lake was the schooner's companionway door, found on the north shore in the fall of the year by Captain Lamphere of the schooner WHITE FISH.

The case of the missing MERCHANT remained dormant for five years, until the summer of 1852 when a group of men coasting from Marquette to the Soo claimed to have sighted the topmasts of the schooner 30 feet below the water's surface in the vicinity of Grand Island. Although plans were made for the relocation and salvage of the wreck, they apparently failed to bear fruit. Considerable excitement was generated when reports were circulated to the effect that among the lost passengers were agents of mining companies who had in their possession some $5,000 in specie, a considerable sum of money in those days. To this date no evidence has been found to indicate that the schooner was ever relocated, identified, or salvaged. So normally ends the story of the MERCHANT, just another vessel that was lost with all hands, in an unknown location in Lake Superior.

However, in this case if we leave the realm of historically verifiable evidence and enter the domain of speculation, some interesting possibilities come to light. Furthermore, if we closely examine the facts thus presented, we can draw some conclusions that might solve the mystery of the MERCHANT, and reveal her present location.

The original evidence that the schooner left the Soo for Portage on the date indicated is undoubtedly true. Contemporary newspaper accounts also agree that on the following day the lake was indeed swept by a fierce gale, one strong enough to have caused the small schooner to founder in the powerful seas.

We can surmise that the MERCHANT was probably overloaded, a not uncommon custom in the days prior to governmental regulations. Her overloaded condition would have made her easy prey for an unexpected gale. Evidence for the overloading was presented by Peter White, one of the founders of Marquette. In later years, White claimed to have sought passage on the fateful trip, but was denied as the schooner was already full. As room for an extra man was commonly made without comment, the schooner must have been full indeed. White also reported seeing the wreck in a dream and that the "passengers and crew are still in the hull and it is in fairly good order."

As the passenger manifest included the three lumbermen headed for L'Anse, the schooner undoubtedly planned a call at that port. The route from the Soo to L'Anse, whether directly or coasting along the south shore, would have carried the MERCHANT past Grand Island at approximately the time the gale struck. The MERCHANT could have foundered outright, simply overwhelmed by the fury of the storm, or she could have elected to seek shelter behind Grand Island, the only refuge for 35 miles in either direction. The MERCHANT could well have foundered while en route to shelter at Grand Island.

The evidence pointing to Grand Island as the location of the sinking is threefold. It was the area of the topmast sighting in 1852, Indian legend claims that a sailing vessel was seen to sink there in a heavy squall at the time of the MERCHANT's disappearance, and Grand Island would be about the right location for the MERCHANT to be at the time of the gale.

If the sighting by the coasting party was correct, we could assume that it was the remains of the MERCHANT they saw, as she was virtually the only sizable vessel lost in Superior to that time. However, the lake can play strange tricks on the eyes when peering down into its shadowy depths. These people may not have seen what they thought they saw!

The recovery of the companionway door on the north shore could not be indicative of a possible location, since it was found so long after the sinking. The fact that no recognizable field of wreckage was ever located should not be considered overly important. At the time lake commerce was extremely light and communication poor. If such wreckage did exist, it might never have been located and even if found, it might never have been recognized or reported. Furthermore, a small schooner, heavily loaded, foundering quickly in a gale would leave precious little evidence. It should also be remembered that no search was initiated until three weeks after the sinking.

After examining all available evidence, two conclusions can be drawn. First, that the MERCHANT's "disappearance" was caused by her overloaded condition coupled with an unexpected gale and second, that her probable location is near Grand Island.

The MERCHANT was one of nine vessels hauled overland around the Soo Rapids in 1845. The others were the schooners SWALLOW, CHIPPEWA, FLORENCE, UNCLE TOM, OCEAN, FUR TRADER, WHITE FISH, and the steamer INDEPENDENCE. Each vessel was placed on rollers much as a house was moved and with both man and beast straining at the lines, was bodily pulled past the roiling waters of the St. Marys. In the MERCHANT's case, it was on to Superior and a place in both history and mystery.

REFERENCES:

Archives, Bayliss Public Library, Sault Ste. Marie, Michigan.

"Autobiography of Captain John G. Parker," *Michigan Pioneer and Historical Collections,* Vol. 30, pp. 582-585, 1905.

Detroit Evening News, June 14, 1884.

"First Trip By Steam to Lake Superior," *Michigan Pioneer and Historical Collections,* Vol. 4, pp. 67-68, 1881.

Lake Superior Journal (Marquette, Michigan), September 8, 1852.

Lake Superior News and Miner's Journal (Sault Ste. Marie, Michigan), July 10, August 14, October 30, 1847.

J.B. Mansfield, *History of the Great Lakes,* Vol. I (Chicago: J.H. Beers, 1899), p. 654.

Mining Journal (Marquette, Michigan), January 28, 1899; August 15, 1904.

Stanley Newton, *The Story of Sault Ste. Marie* (Grand Rapids, Michigan: Black Letter Press, 1907), p. 151.

Reverend John H. Pitezel, *Lights and Shades of Missionary Life: Containing Travels, Sketches, Incidents and Missionary Efforts During Nine Years Spent in the Region of Lake Superior* (Cincinnati: Walden and Stowe, 1883), pp. 126-127.

Ralph D. Williams, *The Honorable Peter White* (Cleveland: Penton Publishing Company, 1907).

Julius F. Wolff, Jr., "They Sailed Away on Superior," *Inland Seas,* Winter, 1973.

SUPERIOR
October 30, 1856

One of the most spectacular and deadly of the Pictured Rocks shipwrecks was the tragic October 30, 1856 loss of the side-wheel steamer SUPERIOR. The 567-ton SUPERIOR was built in Perrysburg, Ohio in 1845 for service between Buffalo and Chicago. The steamer was 191 feet in length, 28 feet in beam (50 feet including the sidewheels) and 11 feet in depth. She was powered by a 180 horsepower, high pressure inclined steam engine that originally was used in the steamer COMMODORE PERRY, launched in 1834. Reusing engines and boilers was common on the lakes during this early period, since two-thirds of the cost of the vessel was for machinery which would easily outlast the wooden hull. The boilers were fired with cordwood, which required frequent refuelling stops.

As typical of the class, she had two decks. The upper was used exclusively for passenger cabins and the lower for crew cabins, cargo, stores and ships' offices. Of the space available in the hull, only one third was free for cargo. Two-thirds were needed for machinery and fuel.

The SUPERIOR became part of a large fleet of steamers that carried immigrants to the new lands in the west. A typical load might include several hundred passengers, various livestock, and miscellaneous freight consisting of anything and everything from buttons to bottles of good sippin' whisky. Her manifests often listed safes consigned to various mining companies on the iron and copper ranges. It is doubtful that these were merely empty safes to be installed in the companies' offices; more likely they were strongboxes carrying hard currency for the payroll. The SUPERIOR quickly earned a reputation as a fast and efficient carrier. The Buffalo Morning Express stated, "We see the steamer SUPERIOR running with larger loads than have ever been carried by any boat on the western lakes."

The steamer also had her share of accidents. In May of 1849, she broke her shaft off Silver Creek, Lake Erie, necessitating several weeks of repair. In October, 1852, also on Lake Erie, she ran into the schooner LOWLAND LASS off Dunkirk, New York. The steamer's effort to tow the schooner to safety failed and the LOWLAND LASS sank in deep water.

The SUPERIOR was sold in the spring of 1853 to Buffalo interests who wanted to run her and the steamer TROY from Cleveland to Toledo. The plan failed and both vessels were sold to Chicago interests the following year. Initially the SUPERIOR sailed from Chicago to various Lake Michigan ports. In the fall of 1855 the SUPERIOR became part of the Lake Michigan and Lake Superior Transportation Company, which had been formed to take advantage of the opportunities presented by the newly opened Soo canal and lock, through which Lake Superior was open to a viable lower lakes connection. The line would become one of the most successful of the upper lakes. A special port of call for the steamer was Superior City, Wisconsin. When the SUPERIOR made its first stop there on May 10, 1856 it provided a critical link with the outside world, important both for commerce and for the morale of the residents of this isolated corner of the lake. Normal time for a run from Chicago to Superior City was four days and six hours. The trip was usually made twice a month.

Under the able command of Captain Hiram J. Jones, the SUPERIOR gained a reputation as a fine sea boat. She was also very popular. It wasn't unusual for Captain Jones to open the large salon for a public dance when in port, if the schedule permitted. When she locked through the Soo on October 28, 1856 everyone expected a routine trip. Since this was likely the last run for the season, it was a very important one for the scattered lake ports on the south shore. These isolated towns depended on the steamer for all outside contact. The last steamer of the season was an emotional event. Whatever supplies it brought would have to last thorough the long, cold winter, until mid-May when the ice cleared enough to let in the first boat.

The best descriptions of the events surrounding the wreck of the SUPERIOR are in the form of statements and letters from some of the survivors. A letter from Joseph W. Dennis, one of the passengers, to the editor of the New York Daily Times provides a vivid account of the disaster. Although it is lengthy, the richness of its detail makes it well worth repeating in full.

"We left the Sault on the morning of Wednesday, the 29th October, weather being favorable until toward night, when it commenced blowing from the northwest, raising a heavy sea. The boat rode very well until 11 1/2 o'clock p.m., when she carried away her rudder, and immediately came round in the trough of the sea. The first sea that struck her afterwards carried away her smokepipes, throwing her freight and cattle down to leeward. The Captain and officers commenced throwing her deck-load overboard. This was found a difficult operation, on account of her being down almost on her beam ends, with heavy gangway planks lashed across her gangways, to keep the

sea out. This had been done previous to her losing her rudder. It was now found that she was making water rapidly. Hands were called to man the pumps, but these were so small as to be of little avail. By 12 o'clock the water had entirely extinguished the fire in her furnaces, the engine stopped, and all hopes of saving her were given up. I then went from the deck to the cabin, to make preparations for going overboard, in case she should sink, as it was evident that she must soon do so. I divested myself of part of my clothing, in order not to be overladen. I then took two life-preservers, which had been thrown aside as useless, on account of the faucets having been rusted. These I tied round me under my coat, securing them by means of a sheet, which I tied over them. About this time the steward and the saloon-keeper began tearing off the doors of the cabin, laying them about so that they might be available for floats. I assisted them until the cabin was stripped on the windward side — the leeward being piled with furniture, stoves, etc. At this time the ladies were lying on the cabin floor, calm and collected, and seemed waiting the event, whatever that event might be.

"At half-past one a cry was heard of 'Rocks! Rocks!' This brought all to their feet, and a rush was made for the boats, there being only two which could be got at; one on the promenade deck, just aft the starboard wheel — the other on the hurricane deck, right above it. The ladies were assisted into these boats by their friends. One young man from Superior City (Stephen Minter by name) had four sisters with him. When I last saw him he was sitting in the middle of a boat, and they were clinging to him in the vain hope that he might save them. Alas! they all found together a watery grave. At this time Capt. Jones came along and said, "You must not do anything rashly; stick by the boat, it is probable she will stand it when she strikes." They then threw over her small anchor, which held her until her stern struck the rocks. The first heavy sea broke her chain, and she came broadside on with a tremendous crash, which caused her to settle down very much.

"Previous to this, I had gone forward and got two stools, with tin cans under them — prepared for life-preservers. On my return through the cabin, I heard the Captain say to some of his crew, "this is the

The last moments of the SUPERIOR.   EDWARD PUSICK

fourth boat I have lost, and it is probably the last." I lashed the stools together by means of a sheet, which I had brought from one of the staterooms — and as soon as she struck I jumped overboard, antici-pating the time of her breaking up, as I saw she must very soon go to pieces. The first sea threw me nearly to the rocks, but its return carried me back. I turned around to look at the wreck, and saw that a heavy sea had carried away the cabin, boats and all, into the water, but the roar of the surf was so terrific as to prevent my hearing anything of the cries of the sufferers. The next sea came down upon me with a heavy load of timbers from the wreck, knocking me senseless and causing me to let go the stools. I sunk, and on coming to found myself strangling, and struggling to reach the surface, which I reached and caught two breaths, when another sea came on laden in the same way. This struck me also, rendering me a second time senseless. When I recovered I found myself lying on my face on the rocks, with a heavy pile of drift-wood upon me. Every sea that came in, however, brought its load, and at the same time lifted the whole mass, so that after a while I was able to extricate myself.

"Hearing voices beyond me, I crawled toward them, and found a number huddled together under the shelving rocks. The place where we were cast was not earth, but was formed of fragments of rocks that had fallen from those that projected over. It was, I should judge, 100 feet long, by 5 broad. We shivered out the night, suffering intensely with the cold, and anxiously looking for daylight. All our efforts for fire proved unavailing. From the time the boat struck I am positive that she did not hold together more than fifteen minutes, before she was piled up on the rocks. At daylight we discovered that her wheels were left where she struck, about 200 feet from where we were, and projecting out of the water about 10 feet. On one wheel five persons were clinging — on the other two — still alive, every sea breaking entirely over them. They called to us for help, but it was of no avail; the sea running so high as to render it impossible, even had we the means within our reach.

"One by one we saw them, poor fellows, drop off, benumbed with cold, and unable to cling longer to this, their "forlorn hope." Among those whom we recognized on the wheels were the second mate, the steward, second clerk, two saloon-keepers, and a fireman. The other we supposed to be a passenger. After passing a miserable day, we built a shanty, as best we could, of pieces of the wreck, wet mattresses, blankets, and pillows, and huddled into it, closely together for warmth.

"We were now eighteen in number. A young lad, of the name of Sisson, under the care of Mr. A.J. Foster, caused us much trouble during the night. Being deranged, he was roaming about, and it was with much difficulty that we could keep him down. On the morning of the second day we found the sea running still heavier than on the evening previous, and watched anxiously for it to subside, as our only chance of escape was by getting off in a boat. In the meantime we subsisted on some raw cabbage and some raisins.

"The wind shifted about noon, and the sea run down almost immediately. We patched up one of the boats which came ashore, and managed to launch it. This was not an easy task, as we were wet, cold and hungry. *Eight of our company got into the boat, the first mate, Mr. Davis, of Detroit, taking charge of her. We proceeded about two miles toward Grand Island, when four of us were landed, viz., the first engineer, one deck hand, one fireman, and myself, getting again very wet and cold, landing through the surf. My feet had now become so swollen, that I was obliged to cut open my boots from the toe to the instep. Mr. Davis left us and returned to the rocks, for the remainder of the party, promising to pick us up in the morning. This was about 4 p.m., and we were to travel on during the night. We started into the woods in hopes of finding a house. We found the snow 16 inches deep, which caused intense pain to our chilled and swollen feet. We wandered through the night along the bank of the lake, finding only perpendicular rocks for some distance. In the morning we came to a small sand beach, near the mouth of Grand Island harbor. Here we saw certain indications that the mate and his party had landed; also, that he had left part of his company and gone away with his boat. We learned, afterward, that he induced them to go ashore, and then left them, privily thinking, probably, that the boat was overladen. This party, so left, started through the woods, down the bay, hoping to find human habitation. Those who were with me, the engineer and his two men, finding that we were left, became disheartened, and said they would stay where they were till succor came, as the boat had taken with her all the provisions, consisting of some flour, some butter, and a few raisins. I left them and proceeded on alone, following in the trail of the men whom the mate had left. After traveling until 2 o'clock p.m. I began to feel extremely faint and weary, having eaten nothing since the night before. I found a few wintergreens which I ate, and some of the inside bark which I pealed from a fir-tree.*

"About noon, Saturday, Nov. 1, I overtook the men who had landed, they having got down off the rocks on to a point of sand, putting into the bay. We were now in sight of a house at the foot of the bay, the distance to which was about two miles across the water, and six or seven around by land, through a dense cedar swamp. These men had given up and laid down, intending to wait till some boat should *come to their relief. I proposed going around the bay that night. To this proposition not one of them would accede at first. After shivering on the sand about two hours and getting a little rested, two of the number concluded to accompany me.*

"We started at 2 o'clock p.m., walking on the beach and wading in the water. We reached the foot of the bay about dark. We had then, I should judge, about four miles to go, but the night was unusually dark and the tangled underbrush and fallen timber rendered the traveling extremely painful and difficult with our swollen feet and exhausted frames. My two companions soon fell behind, so that by 2 o'clock a.m., I heard nothing of them. I was at this time so much exhausted myself as to be unable to travel more than twenty minutes at a time. Then I would sit down and nap. This I scarcely dared to do, fearing that I should be unable to proceed, should I sit too long, or perhaps, that I should not awake at all.

"Painfully, indeed, was the remainder of my journey performed. Alone, far from home and beloved friends, in a bewildering forest, with my feet so swollen and benumbed as to be incapable of feeling, I felt almost at times about to give up. About an hour after daylight, however, I succeeded in reaching the house of Mr. Powell, who immediately took his boat and some provisions and went to look up the scattered suffering party whom I had left behind. He brought them all in, seven in number, in the course of an hour, and never did I behold such a wretched, wo-begone set of human beings. We rejoiced together over our almost miraculous deliverance, but soon the pain, caused by the warmth to our limbs, became almost intolerable. For three days, I suffered the most excruciating pain in my feet. They were black to my ankles, and these were so much swollen as to nearly fill up the legs of my pants. We were treated with the greatest kindness by Mr. Powell and his wife, their kindness seeming to me the more to be appreciated as provisions in those regions are never abundant. On the following Thursday the First Engineer, Mr. Coolahan, with four hands, started for Marquette, 40 miles distant, in order to intercept a boat to take us toward home. At Marquette, Capt. Ryder, of the propeller GEN. TAY-

LOR, heard the story, and came down and took us off. He also picked up the mate and his company, who had made their way to the lighthouse.

"We left Grand Island harbor on Sunday, the 9th, and landed at Detroit on Friday, the 14th Nov. On our arrival at Detroit we were kindly furnished — those who wished to go to Chicago — with passes over the Michigan Central, and myself with one over the Great Western Railroad. On arriving at Buffalo, my home, I called a physician, who pronounced my feet so badly mortified from exposure and chilling as to cause the loss of a part of my toes. This is probably owing to my having traveled one night longer than the rest of the men. I subsequently learned that the boy Sissons and a colored boy died after we had separated. The body of Capt. Jones was brought down to Detroit by the GEN. TAYLOR at the time we came down.

"Words are inadequate to express my joy and gratitude at arriving at my home, where I could procure medical aid, which I had for the past three weeks so much needed. Add to this the sympathy of kind relatives and friends. My physician tells me that I am doing as well as, under the circumstances, can be expected. I have the prospect of being laid up for the winter, but this contrasts favorably with the one which we had at one time contemplated — that of being obliged to remain during that season near the scene of our terrible shipwreck, the horror of which will never, never be obliterated from my memory. The number of the lost, I should compute at about 42."

Joseph W. Dennis

The party in the small boat with Mate Davis made their way to the newly-built lighthouse at the north end of Grand Island in a perilous journey over water and land, described by passenger A.J. Foster:

"Towards noon the second day, the wind lulling and sea running down some, about 4 o'clock we launched the boat with considerable difficulty, owing to our exhausted state. Eight persons got into the boat, and landed one mile and a half distant on the beach. Davis and two others returning, we all got in, making 13, and pulled for Grand

Island, wind blowing fresh out of the harbor, supposed to be six miles off. By the time it was dark we supposed we had got far enough. We landed, after some examination for a landing-place. We got ashore for the purpose of exercise, to keep from freezing. Started again. The wind had increased, and we could not make headway against it, and returned to the place we left. Then three of our men went off into the woods. Davis became alarmed for the boys. For fear of their freezing we concluded to start. We hallooed for the men, but they did not return. We supposed their chances on foot as good as ours in the boat. We started, and found we could not reach Williams' house.

"We made the island about halfway from the light-house to Williams', a rocky shore, and, for fear of freezing, we wished to get on shore, and stamp around and get warm. After rowing about, looking for a place to get up the rocks, we landed and crawled up, and stamped about until morning. Could not see anything, as it was quite dark, and we lost sight of the colored boy and could not find him. When daylight appeared, all, with the exception of the boy Sissons and two men, started to find the light-house, to get assistance. The snow was six inches deep, and it was very hard travelling. A party of them were some distance ahead, and, after travelling about three miles, met Capt. Smith the light-house keeper, coming to our assistance.

"He told me it was only a mile to the house, and he would go and get the men and boy. When he found them the boy Sissons was dead. He brought the two men along with him. We received all the attention in the power of Capt. Smith to give - and as part of the men were able to walk, started for Williams' house, on the harbor side of the island, eight miles distant, to reach some boat or vessel. We arrived at the Light-house on Saturday, Nov. 1, about noon."

Years later another passenger, James Shields, recalled starting on the desperate hike to the lighthouse with a party of 16, seven of whom were blacks. The cold was so intense that after a few hours one "... threw up his arms with a most unearthly yell, staggered and fell dead, the others following at intervals until all perished. Then one by one, the white men followed until but three were left to reach a point from which we called to the lighthouse keeper from the mainland." Luckily, the keeper heard their pleas and sent two Indians with boats to bring them to safety in the warm confines of the East Channel Light. The reference to the seven blacks is fascinating in that it is generally assumed they played no role in early Great Lakes maritime history, especially on Lake Superior.

The survivors did everything possible to fight the terrible cold. When they discovered Captain Jones' body washed ashore in his buffalo coat, they cut off the sleeves and made them into rough shoes.

On her last trip, the SUPERIOR had departed from Chicago on October 25, with a cargo consisting of mining supplies. After clearing the Soo, her next stop was planned to be Marquette, then on eventually to Superior City, Wisconsin. When the news of her disaster reached Marquette nearly a week later, a public meeting was held and money and clothing were collected for the survivors. A special relief party was also sent to the wreck site. Upon their return they reported that everything was battered and torn to pieces against the rocks.

The people of Superior City knew nothing of the disaster until November 18, when a local newspaper voiced concern over its delayed arrival, supposing she, "...has met with some misfortune." Two days later, when smoke from a steamer was sighted far out on the horizon, everyone presumed it was the SUPERIOR. A large crowd gathered at the pier, eager to welcome the long-delayed steamer. But it wasn't the hoped-for SUPERIOR, but the LADY ELGIN, whose Captain Tompkins sadly related the tale of terrible tragedy along the Pictured Rocks. The loss of the SUPERIOR was placed at $25,000, $10,000 for the vessel and $15,000 for the cargo.

There has been a question regarding the number of lives lost. Early newspaper reports listed the names of 36 dead. Dennis gave the number at forty-two, while Mansfield's authoritative History of the Great Lakes states thirty-five lost and sixteen saved. Merchant Steam Vessels of the United States (The Lytle-Holdcamper List) lists thirty-four lost.

As is inevitable following a major disaster, there were many accusations regarding the seaworthiness of the vessel. Some marine men felt she was too old and rotten and never should have been permitted to carry passengers. Visitors to the wreck site reported the vessel being broken to pieces "small enough for kindling wood," and picked up pieces of the boat "so decayed that many of the pieces crumbled into dust on being handled."

The site of the SUPERIOR wreck became a local tourist attraction of sorts, with numerous lake travelers stopping at the area to gawk. One man for whom the wreck seemed to hold a special fascination was William Lemm, the son-in-law of pioneer Grand Island resident Abraham Williams. Lemm was known as a "wrecker," and spent much of his spare time salvaging items from the wreck of the SUPERIOR. He may well have recovered some of the steamer's rumored cargo of mining company payrolls, for after his death the story was often told that, although he had lived alone on the island and held no regular paying job, he had always paid for his purchases in gold!

Other salvagers found tantalizing clues to the SUPERIOR's treasure. In 1883, Captain Michael Beffel of Racine, Wisconsin brought his schooner EXPERIMENT to Lake Superior on a wrecking expedition, salvaging whatever could be recovered from abandoned shipwrecks. While grappling for scrap iron at the site of the SUPERIOR's demise, Beffel and his crew pulled up the door from an old iron-bound

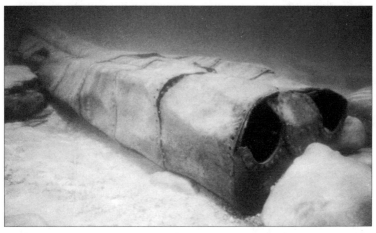

One of the SUPERIOR's boilers.   FREDERICK STONEHOUSE

Deep in the rocks, some small items from the SUPERIOR can still be found.　　　　　　　　　　　　　　　　　FREDERICK STONEHOUSE

oaken safe. When they cleaned it up, they found several dollars in gold and silver coins jammed with sand into the cracks and crevices of the door. The door, with the coins still imbedded in it, was put on public display, and Captain Beffel voiced his intentions of returning to the SUPERIOR "in hopes of recovering something of further value."

Today, the wreckage of the SUPERIOR lies broken and scattered at the foot of the Pictured Rocks. Her remains are spread out for a hundred yards or more around the base of Spray Falls. The most obvious signs of the wreck are the three tubular locomotive-style boilers which lie near the rock pile just west of the falls. The boilers are almost always exposed, even when the rest of the wreck is hidden by the lake's shifting sands, and are easily spotted from the surface. What is left of the proud steamer's hull lies just west of the rock pile, almost up against the cliff. It is usually covered by sand, becoming uncovered only at irregular intervals. More pieces of the wreck, its furnishings and cargo can be found among the rocks and in potholes in the sandstone at depths ranging from 5 feet to 35 feet or more.

COORDINATES: ....46°33.45'N 86°24.91'W
DEPTH: ....5-35 feet

REFERENCES:

Barbeau Papers, Bayliss Public Library, Sault Ste. Marie, Michigan.

Buffalo *Morning Express,* May 26, 1848; May 14, 1849.

Daily Mining Journal (Marquette, Michigan), September 18, 1886.

Duluth Minnesotan, November 22, 1856.

Iron Agitator (Ishpeming, Michigan), August 11, 1883.

C. Patrick Labadie, *Submerged Cultural Resources Study, Pictured Rocks National Lakeshore* (Santa Fee, New Mexico: Submerged Cultural Resources Center, National Park Service, Department of the Interior, 1990), pp. 79-85.

Lake Superior Journal (Marquette, Michigan), November 8, 27, December 12, 1856.

William M. Lytle and Forrest R. Holdcamper, eds., *Merchant Steam Vessels of the United States* (New York: The Steamship Historical Society of America, 1975), pp. 181, 228.

Mansfield, op. cit., p. 677

Milwaukee Journal, February 24, 1935.

Mining Journal (Marquette, Michigan), December 28, 1901; November 22, 1958.

New York Daily Times, November 17, 18, 25, 1856.

A.L. Rawson, "The Pictured Rocks of Lake Superior," *Harper's New Monthly Magazine,* May 1867.

James Shields, *"Wreck of the Steamer SUPERIOR,"* unpublished manuscript, Peter White Public Library, Marquette, Michigan.

Superior Chronicle (Superior, Wisconsin), November 18, 1856.

Herbert Wagner, "Lake Superior's First Major Disaster," *Lake Superior Magazine,* October-November 1991, pp. 58-64.

Samuel Ward, *"Memoirs of Captain Samuel Ward."* Michigan Pioneer and Historical Collections, Vol. 21 (1892) pp. 336-367.

Homer Wells, ed., *"History of Accidents, Casualties, and Wrecks on Lake Superior,"* (manuscript compiled for the U.S. Army Corps of Engineers, Duluth, Minnesota, 1938), p. 3.

ORIOLE
August 9, 1862

The ORIOLE, a 141-foot, 323-ton schooner under Captain Daniel McAdams, departed Marquette at 8 p.m. Friday August 8, 1862 with a cargo of iron ore bound for Erie, Pennsylvania. Aboard were nine crewmen, one passenger, the captain's wife, plus his mother-in-law, for an ominous total of thirteen souls.

The following morning at 7 a.m. the steamer ILLINOIS arrived in Marquette with her bow shattered from keel to upper deck. Her crew told of striking an unknown schooner in the fog off Grand Island Light! When first sighted, the schooner was reportedly running directly towards the steamer, and had she continued on course would have struck the ILLINOIS amidships. The ILLINOIS sheared off and as a result hit the schooner on her quarter.

Questioned by local marine men, the ILLINOIS passengers reported that they had heard screams in the water following the collision and had supposed the schooner had gone down. They severely criticized the steamer's master, Captain Ryder, for not stopping to help the sinking schooner. They also stated that the ILLINOIS was not blowing her fog whistle. Others aboard, including a Bishop McCoskey, claimed that while they did hear voices, they did not judge them as cries for aid.

The mystery concerning the identity of the schooner was solved Monday afternoon when the brig GLOBE, under Captain J.H. Clifford, came into port. Aboard was Andrew P. Fleming of Sodus, New York, the cook of the ORIOLE. The GLOBE had picked up Fleming drifting helplessly in the ORIOLE's yawl about six miles from shore at 8 p.m. Sunday.

Interviewed in Marquette, the cook was in rough shape, with swollen limbs from forty hours exposure and lack of food. In spite of his injuries he was able to tell a damning tale of the disaster. Fleming said he retired at a quarter past midnight on the 8th. At the time the schooner was running in fog, but it wasn't so thick that the signal lamps in the mastheads could not to be seen from deck. On watch were the mate and three sailors. The four other sailors were asleep in the forecastle. The remainder of those aboard were in the aft cabin.

Without warning, at 3 a.m. the steamer struck the ORIOLE on her starboard quarter, cutting directly into Fleming's cabin and literally slicing the schooner in two! When the stern separated as a solid piece, Fleming was thrown into the water. Hanging onto a piece of wood from

The ORIOLE cut in half by the steamer ILLINOIS.
EDWARD PUSICK

the cabin, Fleming looked back and saw the remarkable sight of the schooner still under full sail, but minus her stern! Seeing the steamer about fifty feet away he called for help, but received no answer. Looking back again towards the schooner, he saw it had disappeared into the gray gloom, as had the steamer when next he looked.

For a time he bobbed about in a sea of flotsam, which included several trunks and a half dozen women's dresses. All the while he could hear another voice out in the night. The unknown voice lasted for about an hour and a half, then all was silent.

Shortly after the wreck Fleming also heard the whistle of another steamer apparently following closely in the track of the first. Later he learned this was likely the SEABIRD, which was running behind the ILLINOIS. About 8 a.m. he found the schooner's still-floating stern. Paddling over to it, he crawled aboard and launched the yawl. But without oars, he drifted helplessly for forty hours until picked up by the GLOBE. The stern continued to drift for a considerable period of time. Later it was discovered on the north shore.

The Lake Superior News and Journal, the local Marquette newspaper, severely criticized Captain Ryder of the ILLINOIS for not stopping and rescuing the ORIOLE survivors. The Captain, however, was defended by his clerk who stated that Ryder's first duty was to his vessel and to the safety of the 150 passengers aboard. One of the passengers was no less than the illustrious Mayor Duncan of Detroit.

According to the clerk, the captain's immediate action following the collision was to determine the extent of his own vessel's destruction. After being lowered by rope over the bow to closely examine the damages, Duncan McEachen, an old and experienced sailor, told the captain that they would fill in thirty minutes. Fearing for his passengers, Captain Ryder headed the ILLINOIS towards shore for about twenty minutes, until closer examination showed that he was in no danger of sinking and could safely make Marquette. Meanwhile, the mate on watch at the time of the collision told the captain that the schooner "appeared not much injured." To avoid any panic, the captain kept the knowledge of his damages from his passengers.

Captain Ryder could well have been thinking of another steamer-schooner collision two years before. When the schooner AUGUSTA struck the steamer LADY ELGIN in Lake Michigan in August 1860, an estimated 300 souls went down with the sidewheeler. Most of the passengers were from Milwaukee and it was said this catastrophe left 1,000 of the city's children orphans. It would be hard to believe that Captain Ryder didn't allow the knowledge of this tragety to bear on his decision to run to safety.

The clerk also said the fog wasn't consistent, but rather in banks. Just prior to the accident, the ILLINOIS had left a clear area and thus they were not blowing a fog whistle. Regardless of the explanation, the local bitterness against the ILLINOIS was unchecked.

Off Whitefish Point the propeller BACKUS recovered numerous items including the ORIOLE's wooden secretary containing her books and papers, a quantity of women's clothing, one gold watch, a lady's purse containing $48, some jewelry, and several daguerreotypes of the captain, his wife and children.

Surprisingly, Captain McLeod of the schooner PLOVER discovered part of the schooner's wreck still floating eight miles north of the Pictured Rocks. Climbing aboard and examining the wreck, he reported the "hull was cut in two, with the bottom out and that the sides, masts, spars and part of the deck with sails and rigging were floating on the surface." The hat worn by the captain's wife when she was last in Marquette was the only trace of any person discovered aboard. Captain McLeod said the wreck was one of the saddest sights he had ever seen. He, like many others, was most critical of the performance of the officers of the ILLINOIS.

First officer Thomas Wilson of the ILLINOIS, who had the watch when the collision occurred, had his papers taken immediately following the accident by the Steamboat Inspectors in Detroit. After due investigation, he was exonerated of any blame and his "ticket" was restored in October, 1862.

The schooner, with her cargo of 501 tons of Marquette Range iron ore, was a loss of $17,000.

REFERENCES:

Lake Superior News and Journal (Marquette, Michigan), August 15, 22; September 5, 1862.

Portage Lake Mining Gazette (Houghton, Michigan), August 16, 23, 30; September 13, 1862.

Wells, op. cit., p. 5.

ONEIDA CHIEF
May 31, 1868

The two-masted schooner ONEIDA CHIEF, under Captain Adaim, became a total loss on Au Sable Point after running ashore in heavy weather. Soon after striking she broke in two. Only with great difficulty was the crew able to safely get ashore. She was carrying a cargo of pig iron bound for Cleveland from the Marquette furnaces. The vessel was later stripped of all salvageable gear, and much of her cargo was also recovered. The schooner was an insurance loss of $19,000.

The 127-foot, 252-ton ONEIDA CHIEF was built in 1847 in Clayton, New York by John Oades. She had a relatively uneventful career, although in September 1847 she collided with the schooner PERSEVERANCE off Point aux Barques, Lake Huron. Both vessels were damaged severely enough to require drydocking. During the period 1863-65, she was owned and mastered by Captain Edmond Fitzgerald of Port Huron. He was one of six lake captain brothers and the grandfather of Edmund Fitzgerald, the namesake of the EDMUND FITZGERALD, lost with all 29 hands on Lake Superior November 10, 1975.

REFERENCES:

National Archives, T-279, *(Marine Casualties on the Great Lakes, 1863-1873)*, Records Group 26.

Elizabeth F. Cutler and Walter M. Hirthe, *Six Fitzgerald Brothers, Lake Captains All* (Milwaukee: Wisconsin Marine Historical Society, 1983), p. 215.

Lake Superior Mining and Manufacturing News (Negaunee, Michigan), June 4, 1868.

Lake Superior Mining Journal (Marquette, Michigan), September 5, 1868.

Milwaukee Daily Sentinel, June 3, 5, 22, 24, 29, August 10, 1868.

Wells, op. cit., p. 9.

BERMUDA
October 15, 1870

The cold lake water rushed into the small forecastle with sledge-hammer-like force. It slammed the sleeping crewmen against the hull planks, shocking them into confused consciousness. Their desperate struggles were to no avail. When they climbed into the rat-hole of a forecastle they called home, all was right with the world, but it was here that three of the crew of the BERMUDA met their end.

After all these years, the schooner wreck in Murray Bay remains an enigma. It has variously been identified as the W.W. ARNOLD, GRANADA, DREADNAUGHT and BERMUDA. The best guess though, is that it is the BERMUDA. Although the tale of how the schooner got to Murray Bay is long and unlikely, it still offers the best explanation.

The two-masted BERMUDA was a typical canal schooner, one designed to trade through the confining dimensions of the old Welland Canal between Lakes Ontario and Erie. Launched at Oswego, New York in April 1860, she was 136 feet in length, 26 feet in beam and 11 feet, 9 inches in depth. Her early years were spent in the grain trade between Lakes Michigan and Ontario. When the demand for iron ore increased, she shifted to carrying ore down from Marquette.

During a screaming northwest gale on November 19, 1869 she was driven hard on the reefs at Shot Point, about ten miles east of Marquette. The crew managed to reach the shore safely and her captain walked to Marquette to report the wreck. She was upbound for the city with mining supplies when the accident happened. Although originally feared broken in two, she surprisingly survived the winter and the following summer the wrecking tug MAGNET brought her off the reef and down to Detroit for rebuilding. The yard work cost $800 and included 40 feet of new keel, as well as new bottom planking. She also sported a new paint job: upper works white; waist belt, rail and lower hull green. By late summer 1870, the BERMUDA was back at work.

On September 21, 1870 she left the lower lakes for Marquette with a cargo of general supplies, arriving without incident. After loading 488 tons of ore she departed on October 14, but was overtaken by a gale off Grand Marais. The pounding of the waves caused her to start leaking and her captain brought her to shelter in Munising Bay where she reportedly filled and sank. When she left the docks in Marquette, it was said that she already had two feet of water in her hold. This would certainly cast doubt on both the wisdom of her departure and the quality of her rebuilding in Detroit.

The story goes that Captain Michael Finney beached her near the Anna River, near the present paper mill, making her fast to several trees both fore and aft. Apparently the schooner continued to fill, putting more and more pressure on the mooring lines. At about 8 p.m. the force was so great, it literally ripped the trees off the bank and the BERMUDA suddenly dropped to the bottom. All of her hands were carried down with her. Only the bursting of the cabin deck allowed some of the crew to escape from a watery grave. Three unlucky ones drowned.

Captain Finney and his remaining crew made their way to Marquette and reported their calamity. About a week later they returned to strip the schooner of anything useful and she was abandoned to the insurance underwriters. For practical purposes the BERMUDA just disappeared from the maritime scene.

Thirteen years later, in October 1883, Captain Higgins of the wrecking tug KATE WILLIAMS successfully raised the BERMUDA and towed her into Murray Bay. Once in the bay however, the lifting chains apparently slipped and the schooner settled on the bottom again. The WILLIAMS did manage to remove more than 120 tons of ore, but whether at the Anna River or in Murray Bay isn't known. The following year the wrecking schooner JOHNSON attempted to raise the BERMUDA, but without success. It is likely some additional ore was salvaged.

The confusion regarding her name was added to in a 1901 Marquette Mining Journal article in which a Captain McLeod of Buffalo referred to the Murray Bay wreck as the GRANADA.

In June of 1960 local scuba divers extensively salvaged much of the remaining ore cargo for souvenirs for a regional rock and mineral show.

The Murray Bay wreck provides a near-unique opportunity to study an intact mid-19th century canal schooner. The vessel lies in 25 feet of water in the shelter of the bay, protected from the ravages of Superior's storm waves and the grinding destruction of winter's ice. Consequently, she remains in remarkably good condition; her only major wounds are those inflicted by her salvagers.

All of the vessel's spars and rigging are gone, but the locations of her two masts are still apparent. The foremast hole can be seen about 30 feet from the bow. Her mainmast was stepped in the area where the deck is broken away, but its location can be inferred from the shroud chainplates at either rail.

At the bow, the wreck's bowsprit is missing, giving rise to one source of debate over her identity. The BERMUDA was a fully-rigged schooner, navigating the Great Lakes under sail power alone. As such, she would need to have both bowsprit and jib boom in order to set her jib and flying jib. On the Murray Bay wreck, however, the bowsprit and its bobstay chains and fittings seem to have been neatly removed, as

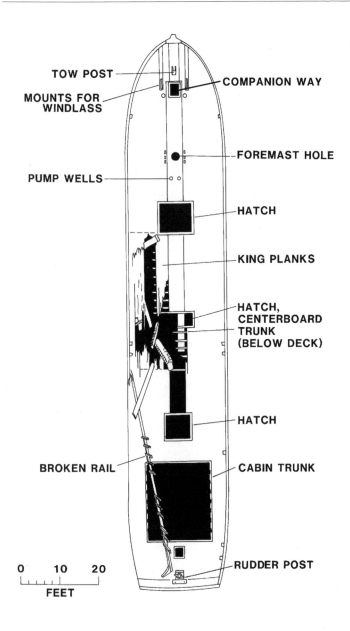

TOW POST

MOUNTS FOR
WINDLASS

COMPANION WAY

FOREMAST HOLE

PUMP WELLS

HATCH

KING PLANKS

HATCH,
CENTERBOARD
TRUNK
(BELOW DECK)

HATCH

BROKEN RAIL

CABIN TRUNK

0 10 20
FEET

RUDDER POST

The BERMUDA as she lies today in Murray Bay.
COURTESY OF THE NPS SUBMERGED CULTURAL RESOURCES UNIT

they might have been on a tow schooner or schooner barge to clear the way for the hawser from her towing steamer.

Near the bow is the massive tow post, known as a samson post. The schooner's man-powered windlass sat behind the samson post, but was removed from the wreck years ago and left to rot on shore near the Munising city dock. The windlass was used to raise the vessel's anchors, and the anchor chains were fed through the two iron chain pipes into the chain locker below. Aft of the foremast hole, two small holes in the deck mark the location of the schooner's hand-operated bilge pumps.

The BERMUDA had three hatches giving access to the cargo hold, as well as two companionways and the large cabin trunk near the stern. The deck between the forward and after hatches is badly broken, probably from the 1883 and 1884 salvage operations. The port rail for some 55 feet at the stern has been torn loose, most likely by modern dive boats before the establishment of the Alger Underwater Preserve and the current system of mooring buoys. What looks like a heavy wooden bulkhead running down the center of the hull and visible through the midships cargo hatch and broken decking is actually the centerboard trunk with the centerboard still raised up in it.

The large rectangular opening near the stern marks the location of the BERMUDA's trunk cabin, which contained the galley and quarters for some of her crew. The cabin was recessed several feet into the deck; the deck beams for the cabin floor can be seen crossing the opening below deck level. Aft of the cabin trunk is a small companionway. A unique ladder consisting of a vertical stanchion with wedge-shaped steps nailed onto it can be seen leading down from this hatch.

At the stern, the rudder stock protrudes up through the deck, capped with an iron crosshead for the "patent" steering mechanism.

Below decks, divers can find what is left of the BERMUDA's cargo of hard, specular iron ore from the Marquette iron range. Also to be seen is one of the schooner's unique features, her inverted hogging arch, an arch of planking running from bow to stern and laid over the interior ceiling planks in order to reinforce the hull. In years past, the bulkheads separating the cargo hold from the forecastle and cabin were still standing. Over the years, diver traffic on the wreck has resulted in the destruction of these bulkheads, as well as the loss of an iron stove and other artifacts which could tell about the sailors' lives. With the establishment of the Underwater Preserve and the education of divers about the cultural importance of shipwrecks, the deterioration of the wreck has slowed dramatically.

LOCATION: . . . . .46°27.88'N 86°38.80'W
DEPTH: . . . . .25 feet

REFERENCES:

Chicago InterOcean, November 8, 1883.

Detroit Free Press, June 23, August 11, October 20, 1870; August 21, 1884.

Iron Agitator (Ishpeming, Michigan), November 10, 1883.

Labadie, op. cit., pp. 35-41.

Mining Journal (Marquette, Michigan), November 20, 1869; July 23, October 29, November 5, 1870; August 16, October 4, 11, 1884; June 11, September 21, 1901.

MARY M. SCOTT
November 2, 1870

The Sand Point area is the site of several shipwrecks and, although it is probably not possible to definitely sort out all of them, among them is the schooner MARY M. SCOTT. Built at Conneaut, Ohio in 1857 by Otis De Wolf, she was named for the wife of one of her owners. Her early days were spent carrying general merchandise, coal and lumber on the lower lakes. The schooner measured 138.6 feet in length, 26.6 feet in beam, 11.8 feet in depth, and 361 tons.

Typical of the times, she experienced her share of adversity. Early in the summer of 1870 she was mauled by a storm off Lake Michigan's

The bones of several vessels are buried in the shifting sands of Sand Point. These may be the remains of the MARY M. SCOTT.

FREDERICK STONEHOUSE

Chambers Island, losing her foresail and three jibs. More serious trouble was yet to come. During a gale on the night of November 2, 1870 the SCOTT, together with the schooner ATHENIAN, tried to reach shelter in Grand Island harbor. The pair had earlier cleared Marquette downbound for Erie with iron ore. The fierce blasts drove both up on Sand Point. The ATHENIAN came off fairly easily, but the SCOTT was on for good. Newspapers reported that she was broken in two and rapidly going to pieces. It is certain however, that at least some of her gear was later salvaged.

The bottom of a canal-size schooner lying in the sandy shallows north of Sand Point is believed to be the wreck of the MARY M. SCOTT. Located 3/8 of a mile northeast of the point proper, the remains consist of the keelson, floor framing, planking, centerboard trunk and part of a cargo of iron ore. The wreckage lies in 10 to 15 feet of water. Although the entire hull is seldom exposed at one time, it

The bones of several vessels are buried in the shifting sands of Sand Point. These may be the remains of the MARY M. SCOTT.

FREDERICK STONEHOUSE

appears to be over 100 feet long and about 24 feet wide. The sternpost projects several feet above the sand, but the rest of the wreckage lies nearly flat on the bottom. Much of the hull bottom is hidden beneath the vessel's iron ore cargo. The ore is a specular hematite with inclusions of iron pyrite, distinctive of the Republic mine on the Marquette iron range. Other small pieces of wooden ship wreckage are scattered across the Sand Point shallows, and many of these are undoubtedly parts of the SCOTT.

LOCATION: . . . . .46°27.54'N 86°36.37'W
DEPTH: . . . . .15 feet

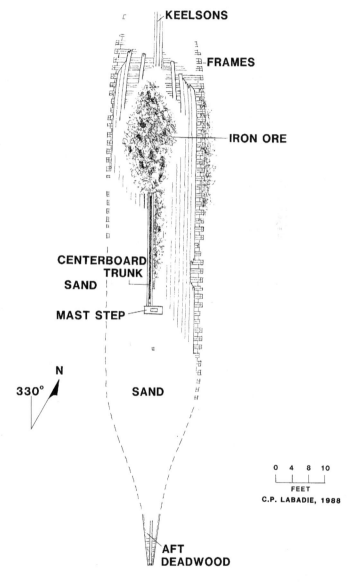

The remains of the MARY M. SCOTT.

C. Patrick Labadie
Courtesy of the NPS Submerged
Cultural Resources Unit

REFERENCES:

Labadie, op. cit., pp. 54-60.

Milwaukee Sentinel, November 9, 14, 1870.

Mining Journal (Marquette, Michigan), October 31, November 5, 1870; December 4, 1886; November 11, 1887.

Munising News, October 21, 1921.

National Archives, T-279, *(Marine Casualties on the Great Lakes, 1863-1873),* Records Group 26.

MARQUETTE
November 13-14, 1872

T he 131-foot, 323-ton, three-masted schooner MARQUETTE under Captain Young was blown high and dry on the sand beach west of Grand Island by a strong north gale during November 13-14, 1872. Although salvage efforts were immediately made, including pumping, dredging and dragging, they failed and the schooner was turned over to the underwriters. The following spring a salvage crew from Detroit attempted to recover her, but discovered the winter storms and ice had destroyed the vessel. Salvage efforts were not completely in vain, since all of the schooner's hardware was recovered.

The MARQUETTE was built at Detroit in 1869 for Captain Allen of Marquette. At the time of her final voyage, she was owned by E.B. Ward. Her final cargo was iron ore.

REFERENCES:

Milwaukee Daily Sentinel, November 22, 23, December 4, 1872, April 18, June 1, 1873.

Mining Journal (Marquette, Michigan), November 23, 30, 1872; April 26, June 7, 1873.

Wells, op. cit., p. 9.

The 131-foot schooner MARQUETTE, wrecked west of Grand Island.
KEN E. THRO

UNION
September 25, 1873

The UNION was a very remarkable vessel. Built in Manitowoc, Wisconsin in 1861 by William and Stephen Bates for the legendary Captain Albert E. Goodrich, it is one of the most unique of the Pictured Rocks shipwrecks. William Bates, famous for his work in developing the American clipper ship, incorporated some very innovative features into the vessel. C. Patrick Labadie, in his Submerged Cultural Resources Study of the Pictured Rocks, stated the propeller, "…included an unconventional hull design with sides that flared outward at the deck level, like an old-fashioned sidewheeler's, a curiously curved stem (bow), and a system of internal reinforcing that enabled him to dispense with the external trusses or arches that were common in that day. The UNION also sported an unusual five-sided pilothouse."

Bates was able to see that wind power was out and steam was the wave of the future on the lakes. If his yard were to prosper, he would have to shift to steam. The high quality of work that Bates did on the UNION impressed Goodrich so much that he awarded the yard the contract for his next vessel, the sidewheeler VICTOR. Later renamed the SUNBEAM, she was lost off the Keweenaw in 1863.

Goodrich is remembered for the excellent Great Lakes fleet that bore his name. From 1856 to 1934, it was the most popular and long-lived line on Lake Michigan.

As was common with many of the vessels of the time, the UNION used the machinery and many of the fittings from another vessel, the wooden propeller OGONTZ, also a Goodrich boat. Built in 1848, the OGONTZ was never a successful vessel, lacking in dependability. Sold and converted to a sailing vessel, she earned her way only a short time, foundering in a Lake Michigan gale in 1862.

The UNION was the first steamer built in Manitowoc and the activity in the Bates yard created much public interest. Her launching on April 26, 1861 was attended by hundreds of people, many coming from far and wide around the entire county to see the colorful and

The old propeller UNION. Her bones lie somewhere on Au Sable Reef.
C. PATRICK LABADIE

exciting affair. When she hit the water, a large flag bearing her name unfurled at the mast. For a nation just entering the second year of the Civil War, the name was most appropriate.

The 434-ton vessel measured 163 feet, five inches in length, 26 feet in beam and 10 feet, nine inches in depth. A double decker, she had cargo space below and between decks while a full-length passenger cabin ran the length of the promenade deck. She cost an estimated $19,000.

Goodrich ran his new propeller under charter to the Great Western Railway Line between Chicago and Sarnia. Passengers and general freight went west, and barreled flour went east. On August 1, 1862, Goodrich sold the UNION to two Sheboygan, Wisconsin men who continued her on the same run. In 1866 she changed hands again and was placed in the Lake Superior trade. Starting at Chicago, she went to Superior City, with intermediate stops at Mackinac, Sault Ste. Marie, Marquette, Houghton, Hancock, Copper Harbor, Eagle River,

Ontonagon, Bayfield and LaPointe. In total she made 13 round trips to Lake Superior that year. During the next four years the same service was maintained with only occasional exception. In April, 1864 she was sold to Lewis Curtis of Sheboygan and Mary L. Rice of Chicago. Curtis held two-thirds interest and Rice one-third. In 1871 she was back on the Chicago - Sarnia route.

By then she was getting on in years for the passenger trade. Bigger, newer, fancier, more comfortable boats were the norm. The UNION's days as a passenger ship were numbered.

Following the 1871 season, the Curtis interest in the UNION was sold to Mark English of Green Bay, Wisconsin. English owned a Green Bay foundry and planned to use her exclusively to bring Marquette ore down to his mill. To accommodate the new role, her cabin was cut in two and a large piece of it removed, leaving a small pilothouse forward and an engine house and cabin aft. The tonnage was adjusted to 341.

For the 1872 season she was deeply involved in the Marquette ore trade. Like any hard working vessel, the UNION had her share of scrapes. Early in the season she went aground on Strawberry Reef in Green Bay but was hauled off without trouble. In June she and her tow, the schooner CASCADE, went ashore during a dense fog on Laughing Whitefish Point Reef, 18 miles east of Marquette. Both were easily recovered. During the season she managed to complete 11 round trips to the Marquette docks.

On September 25, 1873 the UNION was bound down from Marquette under the command of Captain D.L. Stearns with a cargo of 432 tons of ore when she was overtaken by a strong northwest gale. Driven south of her intended course by the powerful gusts, she ran hard up on Au Sable Reef at 4 a.m. Captain Stearns quickly dumped his deck load in an effort to get off, but just when it looked like he would succeed, the wind shifted and pushed him farther onto the rocks. When it was evident all was lost he got his crew off safely. The UNION was far too exposed and the weather too rough for the old propeller to survive. When the captain returned several days later, she was already breaking up.

The following year the sidewheeler J.K. WHITE recovered the machinery from the wreck. In 1875 another boiler, reportedly badly dented, was recovered and taken to Grand Island. The UNION was a loss of $18,000.

Some wooden hull wreckage about a half mile east of the Au Sable Light and 200 yards offshore may be from the UNION. Other sections of the vessel could probably be found nearby.

REFERENCES:

Chicago InterOcean, August 31, 1874.

Detroit Free Press, March 12, 1861; June 16, 1872.

James L. Elliott, *Red Stacks Over the Horizon* (Grand Rapids, Michigan: William Eerdmans Publishing, 1967), pp. 26, 37.

Labadie, op. cit., pp. 132-136.

Milwaukee Daily Sentinel, September 30, October 9, 1873; August 18, 31, 1874.

Mining Journal (Marquette, Michigan), October 4, 1873.

Lytle and Holdcamper, op. cit., p. 218.

Wells, op. cit., p. 10.

F. MORRELL
November 7, 1874

One schooner wreck that has nearly been obliterated by Lake Superior is that of the F. MORRELL. The 144-foot, 369-ton schooner departed Marquette with a cargo of 617 tons of iron ore on November 7th. That night, during a heavy gale, she went hard on the rocks near the northwest corner of Grand Island. The crew all got safely ashore, but the wreck went to pieces two days later. The F.

MORRELL was owned by Peter Wex of Buffalo and her master, John Mullins. The loss of the schooner and cargo was placed at $23,000.

Captain Mullins later said the weather was very thick and he only sighted the island moments before his vessel struck. The cargo was owned by the Kloman Iron Company and consigned to Erie interests. The Marquette-based tug J.K. WHITE later stripped the wreck of all salvageable items. The WHITE was back at the wreck the following summer, apparently recovering as much of her ore as possible.

What may be the remains of the MORRELL lie scattered in 15 feet of water off the northwest corner of Grand Island. One shallow pocket in the sandstone holds a layer of iron ore, along with capstans, chains, and other fittings from an old sailing vessel. Near the ore pile, the sandstone bottom is scored with a series of grooves, carved by the iron bolts of a section of wooden hull that must have lain there for years, moving back and forth in the surf. Divers have reported finding wire rope rigging and other shipwreck artifacts farther south along the shore of Grand Island, but no surviving portions of the hull have yet been discovered.

The F. MORRELL. She wrecked on the west side of Grand Island.
KEN THRO

LOCATION: ....46°32.85'N 86°42.88'W
DEPTH: ....15 feet

REFERENCES:

Chicago InterOcean, November 11, 1874.

Detroit Evening News, November 12, 1874.

Milwaukee Daily Sentinel, November 12, 1874.

Mining Journal (Marquette, Michigan), November 14, 1874, June 26, 1875; November 11, 1887.

Stonehouse Files.

CHENANGO
November 20, 1875

One wreck that occurred as an indirect result of the charcoal iron industry in the village of Onota (now called Christmas) was the 384-ton schooner-barge CHENANGO. She left Marquette with a cargo of 500 tons of iron ore for the Bay Furnace in the mid-afternoon of Saturday, November 20th in tow of the tug JAY C. MORSE. By 6 p.m. both vessels were engulfed in a thick snow squall accompanied by increasing seas, making it dangerous to attempt to enter the west channel. The tug tried to turn around and take her tow back to safety in Marquette, but in the rolling seas the schooner had become unmanageable. The MORSE cut her free and ran into Grand Island Harbor alone. The CHENANGO attempted to sail through the narrow channel between Wood and Williams Islands but miscalculated and struck the reef.

In the morning the crew aboard the tug could see the CHENANGO hard aground on the reef, with her sails still set and the seas washing completely over her. With the temperature below zero, the schooner was covered with a solid mass of glistening ice. The MORSE tried to go to the CHENANGO's assistance, but the heavy seas still running prevented her from getting near the schooner. They could see no sign of anybody on board the wreck, and the yawl was gone from its davits, so they assumed the crew had tried to escape in the boat and drowned.

By Monday morning, the storm had subsided enough that the tug was finally able to reach the schooner, where they were amazed to find the crew alive, huddled in the galley! When the CHENANGO first grounded on the reef, following seas had smashed in her stern and ripped the yawl from its davits, trapping the crew aboard. Captain Ferris, his wife, the mate and three sailors took refuge in the galley, reinforcing the after bulkhead with whatever timbers they could lay their hands on to keep the waves from washing into their crude shelter. They spent the next 35 hours shivering in the cramped galley, fearing that each wave that slammed into the wreck would tear the cabin away. When they finally emerged onto the deck, they found the hull and rigging nearly a solid mass of ice. Small ropes were coated with ice to the size of a man's wrist.

The CHENANGO was abandoned where she lay, a loss of $16,000 to her owner, Captain Ferris. The next summer the Bay Furnace Company salvaged most of the ore from the shallow wreck.

The remains of the CHENANGO lie in 10 feet of water a few hundred yards southwest of Wood Island. The wreckage comprises most of the bottom of the vessel's hull. The boat's wooden rudder can be found in the same general area, and a large wooden-stock anchor believed to be from the CHENANGO was recovered from the lake bottom near the island before the area became an underwater preserve.

The tug JAY C. MORSE was a veteran of shipwreck on Lake Superior. On July 13, 1867 she was carrying a group of excursionists when the tug struck a reef near Marquette. Two lady passengers were thrown overboard by the impact and three men leapt in to rescue them. The ladies were quickly pulled back aboard, but one of the rescuers drowned. To prevent its sinking, the tug was beached in shallow water to await repair. The MORSE again met misfortune in 1889. She capsized and sank when she ran too close to the bank in the Portage Ship

Canal in an attempt to avoid striking another steamer. The MORSE was again recovered.

LOCATION: . . . . .46°30.10'N 86°44.76'W
DEPTH: . . . . .15 feet

REFERENCES:

Cleveland Plain Dealer, August 5, 1889.

Milwaukee Daily Sentinel, November 23, 24, 1875; June 14, 1876.

Mining Journal (Marquette, Michigan), November 27, 1875.

Wells, op. cit., p. 11.

ANNIE COLEMAN
July 19, 1879

The small lower lakes schooner ANNIE COLEMAN met her end at the mouth of the Hurricane River. Under Captain George Wilson, she was upbound for Marquette when she ran hard on the rocks during a dense fog. Left with no other choice, Captain Wilson and his crew spent three days hiking the 70 miles to Marquette to report the casualty. The schooner was a total loss of approximately $10,000.

REFERENCE:

Mining Journal (Marquette, Michigan), July 26, 1879.

STARLIGHT
September 29, 1880

The small schooner STARLIGHT, employed to carry railroad supplies to the camps of the Detroit, Munising and Marquette Railroad, then under construction, departed Marquette on Tuesday, September 28. She successfully arrived at the camp at Sucker Bay, her first stop, and unloaded part of her cargo. According to later accounts in the local newspaper, the crew then proceeded to celebrate the success of their long voyage with the heavy use of intoxicants.

They must have spent some considerable time celebrating since, by the time they finally departed, a stiff northwester was blowing. Recognizing the danger, the railroad men urged them not to leave, but the fearless men paid no heed. When the STARLIGHT sailed out into the lake, she carried not only her three man crew, but also two Swedish railroad workers.

Concerned when the STARLIGHT failed to reach Munising, a Mr. Hendrie, one of the railroad men, organized a search party. His efforts were successful as searchers soon found some pieces of the boat, including her sails and masts as well as several items from her cargo on the beach. On Sunday, her hull was discovered floating upside down near Au Train.

About three weeks later the body of the STARLIGHT's captain, Elmo Larmo, washed ashore on Grand Island. Searching his pockets for positive identification, his pocket watch was discovered, which ominously had stopped at 7 p.m., the time it was surmised the STARLIGHT swamped in the seas. His was the only body ever recovered.

REFERENCES:

Detroit Evening News, October 5, 1880.

Mining Journal (Marquette, Michigan), October 2, 9, 30, 1880.

Weekly Agitator (Ishpeming, Michigan), October 30, 1880.

MARY JARECKI
July 4, 1883

The MARY JARECKI was another victim of the infamous Au Sable fog god. The 179-foot steam barge with her iron ore cargo was en route from Marquette to the Soo on Wednesday, July 4th, when she drifted south of her intended course in the fog and ran ashore at full steam about a mile and half west of Au Sable Point. The force of the impact drove her bow nearly three feet out of the water!

Captain Anthony Everett of Kenosha, in an attempt to save his charge, immediately went to the Soo to secure the tug MYSTIC with a lighter and steam pump. The salvage efforts were fruitless. They tried pumping all day Saturday but try as they might, the water in the hull could not be lowered a single inch. Apparently the JARECKI was holed too badly. She was also pushed up amidships, probably broken, and her boiler had shifted. The owners readily gave her up to the underwriters.

The steam barge MARY JARECKI (center) iced in at Escanaba circa 1875-76. The vessel on the right is the M.R. WARNER.

C. Patrick Labadie

Later in the month the tug OSWEGO and lighter VAMPIRE, with large steam pumps, heavy hawsers and a diver, departed Detroit for the wreck. Arriving at the broken steamer, the diver did what he could to stop up the leaks in her bottom. Four large steam pumps were then set to work for three days and two nights, but could not lower the water enough to float the crippled vessel. The salvors gave up, stripped her of her rigging and abandoned her.

The next month, local salvagers tried their hand at raising the steamer. In August the Marquette Mining Journal reported, "The wrecking tug KATE WILLIAMS has been at work on the wrecked propeller MARY JARECKI for the past couple of weeks and she may have got off by this time. The tug was provided with a full wrecking outfit and a force of divers. The bottom was found to be in a badly damaged state, being pounded full of bad holes, which the divers were patching up at the last report we had from there. When this was done, six large steam pumps were to be set to work pumping the water out of her and an attempt then made to raise her with pontoons. The captain in charge anticipated no difficulty in raising her and thinks that he will deliver her at the dry docks in a short time."

The optimism of the salvagers was grossly misplaced. The MARY JARECKI clung to the bottom with quiet desperation. Finally giving up, the insurance company offered her up for sale as is. There were no takers. Eventually the wreckers recovered virtually all of the machinery, related tackle and rigging and much of her cargo. A storm in September finally destroyed the vessel.

More than a century of Lake Superior storms have continued the destruction of the MARY JARECKI. Her remains are scattered in shallow water a mile and a quarter west of the Au Sable Lighthouse, near the Hurricane River. About 200 yards east of the river's mouth, a 140-foot piece of the bottom of a bulk freighter lies in shallow water just 50 feet offshore. This most likely belongs to the ill-fated vessel. A hundred yards east of this section, another piece of wreckage, probably part of her side, lies in the surf line. Offshore from this section of hull are some pieces of her broken-up boiler. Other pieces of wreckage, including piping and sheets of steel, lie in 15 to 20 feet of water nearby.

The MARY JARECKI was built in 1871 at Toledo by Bailey Brothers for Shepard, Henry & Company of Erie. She was named in honor of the wife of one of the owners. Officially she measured 179.6 feet in length, 32.7 feet in beam, and 13.2 feet in depth with a gross tonnage of 502.3. Power was provided by a single-cylinder, non-condensing, high pressure steam engine with a 27-inch cylinder and 32-inch stroke. The hull was towed to Detroit for installation of the machinery. The Detroit Free Press reported, "She is one of the staunchest steamers ever built at Toledo. Her cabin is on the upper deck which extends about one-third the length of the boat. It is furnished in good style, is large and well arranged and will afford comfortable quarters for the officers and about 40 passengers. Her fuel will be carried on deck, leaving her hold clear for ore. She has also been provided with sails. She is painted green with white upper works and carries two masts." She was valued at $46,000.

Her owners were major coal and iron ore shippers and their new steamer was immediately put on the Escanaba - Erie route. It was coal up and ore down.

The MARY JARECKI had her share of accidents. She went up on the shoals off Summer Island, Lake Michigan during a fog on October 30, 1872. After lightering part of her cargo, she was released. On October 5, 1874 she and her barge, the M.R. WARNER, went ashore at Lake Huron's Rock Falls. The accident was blamed on blinding, choking smoke from forest fires that caused her to lose her course. She was released a week later, but needed $2,000 in repairs. A collision on Halloween 1874 in the St. Clair River, off Marine City, between the upbound JARECKI and the downbound schooner MAGELLAN resulted in only minor damage to the schooner but a twisted stem for the steamer.

The life of a vessel in the ore trade was a hard one and in 1879 she was rebuilt in Erie. A second deck was added, increasing her cargo capacity to 1,200 tons and gross tonnage to 645.65.

Shepard, Henry & Company sold the steamer to John R. Barker of Chicago in 1880. Together with the barge C.A. KING, she started a new career hauling ore from Marquette to Milwaukee. Three years later, the MARY JARECKI met her end at Au Sable point.

LOCATION: . . . . .46°40.15'N 86°10.07'W (Boiler)
DEPTH: . . . . .6 feet (Boiler)

REFERENCES:

Chicago InterOcean, October 31, November 5, 1872; October 8, 9, 13, 1874; October 10, 1880; July 10, 1883.

Detroit Free Press, May 13, 1871; May 11, 1873; July 14, 1883.

Labadie, op. cit., pp. 95-104.

Log of Au Sable Light Station, July 4 - September 25, 1883, National Archives, Records Group 26.

Mining Journal (Marquette, Michigan), July 14, 28, August 25, November 24, 1883; July 4, 1884.

Toledo Blade, November 3, 1874.

Wells, op. cit., p. 14.

WABASH
November 16, 1883

The tug SAMSON was en route to Marquette towing the coal-laden schooner-barges WABASH, C.G. KING and C.H. JOHNSON when she hit a heavy northeast gale accompanied by snow off the Pictured Rocks. During the height of the storm the tow cable to the WABASH broke. Soon the powerful waves drove the schooner-barge aground off Chapel Beach. The pounding waves broke the schooner in two places, forward and aft of the mainmast. The crew stayed aboard throughout the long, stormy night, suffering greatly from the drenching spray and freezing weather. Although the next morning they were able to reach safety in a makeshift raft, they were stranded without food or shelter until the following day when they were finally picked up by a small boat from the SAMSON

During the storm the JOHNSON also lost her tow line. Only skillful handling by her captain, William Parker, and a healthy dose of good luck kept her from joining the WABASH. Before Parker could haul her off into the safety of the open lake, the schooner was driven to within 100 feet of the towering, wave battered cliffs. Although she survived this time, twelve years later the C.H. JOHNSON was blown ashore and became a total wreck at Gros Cap in the Straits of Mackinac.

The 680-ton, two-masted WABASH, a casualty of $15,600, was fully insured, including her cargo of 660 tons of coal. She measured 140 feet in length, 26 feet in beam and 12 feet in depth and was launched in Toledo in 1873.

The same storm that ended the WABASH's days also spelled the end for the steamer MANISTEE. The MANISTEE had departed Ontonagon en route for Portage (today Houghton-Hancock), never to arrive. A field of wreckage west of the Keweenaw provided the only clue to the loss of the steamer and the fate of the 23 people aboard.

The shifting sands off Chapel Beach occasionally reveal part of the broken hull of the WABASH, about 50 yards off the middle of the beach in eight feet of water. Nearly the entire bottom of the hull is there, but often only the keelson and perhaps a few frames can be seen. Farther offshore pieces of wooden framing and chunks of coal from her cargo can be found scattered in 16 to 48 feet of water.

LOCATION: . . . . .46°32.86'N 86°26.80'W (Hull)
46°33.65'N 86°26.30'W (Frames)

DEPTH: . . . . .8 feet (Hull) 48 feet (Frames)

REFERENCES:

Charles E. Feltner and Jeri Baron Feltner, *Shipwrecks of the Straits of Mackinac* (Dearborn, Michigan: Seajay Publications, 1991), pp. 74-78.

Iron Agitator (Ishpeming, Michigan), November 24, 1883.

Mining Journal (Marquette, Michigan), November 24, 1883.

Wells, op. cit., p. 14.

EMMA A. MAYES
May 10, 1884

During the fall of 1883 the tug MUSIC, towing the schooner-barges NELSON, FORSTER, RICHES and EMMA A. MAYES was steaming from Buffalo to Prince Arthur's Landing (today Thunder Bay). Near Au Sable Point, the small fleet ran into a heavy north gale. Seeking shelter from the rough weather, the tug brought her charges to Grand Island.

Since all of the barges were leaking badly and it was late in the season, the MUSIC left them in Trout Bay and returned to Bay City with the crews for the winter. Leaving barges to winter at Grand Island was not at all unusual. Normally the vessels would be grounded as close inshore as possible and anchored for safety.

The first week in May 1884, the MUSIC returned to continue the trip. After the crews re-rigged the barges and pumped them out, the tug nudged them off their winter perches and reassembled its tow.

On Saturday, May 10, the MUSIC and her tows departed Grand Island. The lake was still filled with large floating chunks of ice and the vessels were constantly brushing into them. About seven miles out, a large piece of ice struck the MAYES forward, staving in her old and rotten hull. Quickly the MAYES filled and sank bow first in an estimated 200-300 feet of water. She went down so fast her master, Captain Leander Bennett, and his eight man crew barely had time to escape. The barge and her cargo of 850 tons of stove coal were a total loss of $9,000. Neither was insured. The MAYES was owned by Mitchell and Boutell of Bay City.

REFERENCES:

Ashland Press, May 24, 1884.

Bay City Evening News, May 12, 14, 1884.

Mining Journal (Marquette, Michigan), November 24, 1883; May 17, 1884.

Thunder Bay Sentinel (Port Arthur, Ontario), May 23, 1884.

Wells, op. cit., p. 14.

SMITH MOORE
July 13, 1889

The most famous shipwreck in the Pictured Rocks area is that of the SMITH MOORE, lost in the Munising east channel on July 13, 1889 as the result of damages suffered in a collision. The 1,191-ton wooden steamer was built by the Globe Iron Works in Cleveland in 1888 and was partly owned by Harvey Brown of that city. Captain Smith Moore of Marquette was a half owner. The steamer's dimensions were 223.4 feet in length, 35 feet in beam and 18.2 feet in depth. Construction costs were approximately $90,000.

As in the ORIOLE disaster of 1862, the first news of an accident reached Marquette only when the other vessel involved, in this case the 223-foot wooden steamer JAMES PICKANDS, docked. When the PICKANDS arrived at 9 a.m. on the 14th, a number of deep abrasions could be plainly seen on her port bow. Some of the half-inch thick steel reinforcing plates were ripped open for nine feet!

Captain Clinton Ennis of the PICKANDS, on watch at the time of the accident, stated that at 4 a.m. on the 13th, he was approximately ten miles off Grand Island and running in a fog. Visibility was about 100 yards and his fog whistle was blowing. He heard a second horn, but the

The steam barge SMITH MOORE.　　MARQUETTE MARITIME MUSEUM

fog played tricks with the sound and he couldn't determine its direction. Suddenly the massive bow of another steamer came into view barely 75 yards ahead and slightly to port. The second vessel sighted him at the same time and signaled for a starboard crossing. Captain Ennis put his wheel hard over but still struck a glancing blow to the other vessel, now recognized as the SMITH MOORE. Since the PICKANDS was light (without cargo), she bounced off. Ennis slowed and waited for a signal from the MOORE, but none came so he proceeded to Marquette, thinking the damage slight. He couldn't have been more wrong!

About 10 a.m., observers in Munising, including the keeper of the East Channel Light, witnessed a most unusual sequence of events. Two steamers appeared, rounding Trout Point and heading for the harbor, one vessel towing the other. About 300 feet shy of the sand spit that partially blocks the channel, the lead vessel cut loose the tow line and took the crew off the disabled steamer. Five minutes later the second vessel sank. The curious lightkeeper as well as others rowed out and discovered the sunken vessel to be the SMITH MOORE. Her masts were standing a full fifteen feet clear of the water and much of her upper works which broke off during the sinking were floating nearby.

The SMITH MOORE, under Captain Morrison, had departed Marquette at 2 a.m., July 13, bound for Cleveland with a cargo of 1,743 tons of iron ore. The steamer carried a crew of fifteen plus several passengers, including the wives and daughters of the captain and first mate.

Captain Morrison later stated he had sounded two whistles when he saw the PICKANDS and when she didn't alter course, blew two more. The PICKANDS struck heavily, cutting deeply into his bow. Water poured in through the immense hole. He knew at once it was only a matter of time before she sank.

Immediately after the collision, the SMITH MOORE began blowing distress signals, but the PICKANDS never responded. The captain ordered all steam put on the engine, the lifeboats made ready, and her course set for Grand Island. Hearing the distress signals from nearly five miles away, the 201-foot steamer M.M. DRAKE came to her assis-

The SMITH MOORE on the way to the bottom.   EDWARD PUSICK

tance. She took off the sinking steamer's passengers and crew and, after putting a line aboard, started the tow for Munising. The DRAKE had left Marquette shortly after the MOORE.

Several weeks following the wreck, the sunken SMITH MOORE was inspected by hard hat commercial divers in an attempt to determine if salvage was possible. Captain Dennis Sullivan, the wrecking master of the Milwaukee-based Commercial Union Insurance Company, visited her with diver John Quinn. After inspecting the wreck, Quinn reported she was level in 90 feet and her hull was in good shape, but that her stern cabin and pilothouse were gone. Evidently they had been blown off when she foundered as the lightkeeper noted. Her masts were still upright and, judging from the green paint scrapes on one, had already been grazed by a passing vessel.

Due to the nature of the cargo, soft ore which turns to a putty-like consistency when wet, making it very difficult to work with, it was considered uneconomical to salvage her. The death sentence was passed on the SMITH MOORE.

As circumstance would have it, Captain Morrison and Captain Ennis did have an opportunity to discuss the unfortunate accident. Both captains met at the Soo Canal while downbound. Reportedly the dialogue was both vehement and "raw."

The SMITH MOORE was known as a fast steamer. In May of 1886, under a Captain White, she broke her own record from Cleveland to Marquette and return. From lighthouse to lighthouse she made the trip in five days, fifteen hours and ten minutes. The time included four hours to load and trim a cargo of 1,500 tons of ore. It was more normal, however, if she averaged seven trips in 60 days.

The SMITH MOORE was named for Captain Smith Moore. Captain Moore was the master of the steam barge H.B. TUTTLE until July of 1880, when he resigned to take command of his "own" ship. How long Captain Moore remained in command of the MOORE is difficult to determine, but by July of 1886 he had changed vessels and was ironically the captain of the JAMES PICKANDS. The PICKANDS was also known as a fast ship.

Captain Moore was by any standard an enterprising man. He owned the popular Marquette hotel, The European House. While developing a residential plat in Marquette in 1884, he discovered a gold mine and founded the Euclid Gold Mining Company. Moore vigorously promoted the mine for several years, but it never became a financial success.

The SMITH MOORE's first visit to the Marquette docks was in early September of 1880. Locally she was hailed as "one of the finest barges in the ore trade" and remained a popular vessel in the area. In July of 1881 she took a load of excursionists from Marquette on a day trip to view the famous Pictured Rocks. Another outing included a picnic basket lunch on Williams Island.

The SMITH MOORE was nearly lost to fire in 1884. She was discharging an ore cargo in Sandusky when a fire broke out in the port. The steamer only escaped by wetting down and cutting away all of her smoldering rigging.

There are a number of ironies in the entire SMITH MOORE story. For example, the PICKANDS later became a victim of Lake Superior shipwreck. On September 27, 1894, she ran off course in a smoke haze and struck Sawtooth Reef off the Keweenaw's Eagle River, becoming a total loss. In a twist of fate, at the time of the PICKANDS - SMITH MOORE collision, the PICKANDS was owned by Captain John T. Moore of Cleveland. And of course, there is the fact that the PICKANDS was for a time mastered by Smith Moore. The M.M. DRAKE, the rescuer of the SMITH MOORE, sank in a vicious Lake Superior gale off Vermilion Point on October 2, 1901.

The wreck has also been the scene of latter day tragedy and romance. At least one scuba diver has been killed while exploring her secrets. On May 24, 1992, two Lansing, Michigan divers were married on her deck with local charter boat captain Peter Lindquist presiding. Full face masks and underwater communication devices provided the method for the appropriate exchange of vows.

The SMITH MOORE wreck was first found by scuba divers in 1966. A group from Grand Rapids, together with a Detroit group, were reportedly seeking the steamer's mythical cargo of 350 barrels of whiskey and 150 barrels of silver ore. The vessel's actual cargo, of course, was iron ore and nothing more, but the truth has never deterred a treasure hunter! Early divers stripped the vessel of many artifacts, including her bell and steam whistle. Another group salvaged her anchors.

Today the wreck of the SMITH MOORE is one of the star attractions of the Alger Underwater Preserve, and is visited by hundreds of divers each year. The wreck lies a quarter mile south-southwest of the green bell buoy in the east channel, and is usually marked by several mooring buoys. Maximum depth on the wreck is about 95 feet, with the deck at 85 feet.

The wreck lies nearly intact on the sand bottom. The cabins are missing, a section of decking over the cargo hold is broken, and the bow and foredeck are damaged, but otherwise the MOORE is extremely well preserved. The damage at the bow resulted in the 1960's when a group of divers used a large amount of dynamite in an attempt to remove one of the MOORE's anchors. Besides severing the anchor chain, the explosion also split the bow at the stem and blew the foredeck completely off the boat. The foredeck flipped upside down and fell back into the shattered bow. Divers can find the bow capstan still in place on the inverted foredeck, next to an old wooden wheelbarrow once used to handle cargo aboard the steamer.

Great Lakes sailors, like their saltwater brethren, were very superstitious and the crew of the SMITH MOORE was no exception. To ensure good luck for their vessel, they nailed up a horseshoe in a prominent location on the stem of the vessel. For years divers could see this talisman still in its place in the splintered bow, but in 1988 a vandal stole the horseshoe, leaving only its rusty outline on the stem. Perhaps the horseshoe never did bring good luck to the MOORE since, contrary to tradition, the shoe was mounted with its open end down, allowing the luck to "run out."

On the intact deck aft of the damaged area, the sills of the cabin bulkheads can be seen on the deck. The lightly-constructed deckhouses were blown off by the rush of air escaping the sinking steamer.

In the midsection of the SMITH MOORE are her six cargo hatches. Aft of the first and fourth hatches are the stumps of two of the vessel's three masts, encircled by the fiferails. A third mast was stepped between the boiler house and the engine. Although steam provided most of the motive power, sails could be set to catch favorable winds, both to save fuel and to add to her speed. The masts broke off after the sinking, and lie buried in the sand near the wreck. One of her foresail spars, either the boom or the gaff, lies in the cargo hold in the area of broken decking on the starboard side.

Just ahead of the sixth cargo hatch is the vessel's steam winch, which was used to pull taut the mooring lines. The winch's steam engine also powered the twin bilge pumps on either side of the winch. A hand-powered pump sits on deck on the other side of the cargo hatch, just ahead of the iron boiler house.

A diver swims through the SMITH MOORE engineroom prior to the wreck being sanded in.

FREDERICK STONEHOUSE

A diver next to one of the SMITH MOORE propeller blades. At this writing, the propeller is buried in the sand bank.

FREDERICK STONEHOUSE

A diver uses an air lift to try to clear the wreck of the slowly encroaching sand. FREDERICK STONEHOUSE

Aft of the boiler house, the main steam pipe and throttle valve lead to the SMITH MOORE's two cylinder fore-and-aft compound steam engine. Only the tops of the cylinders are visible in the engine trunk. The massive timber projecting out of the deck aft of the engine is the samson post or tow post for the tow line to the steamer's consort. Alongside the samson post is the stern capstan. A rack on the starboard bulwark held the wooden handles used by the crew to turn the capstan. The rudder stock projects up through the deck, and the removable emergency steering tiller lies nearby.

Up until 1986, divers could swim over the stern and down to the steamer's rudder and massive iron propeller at a depth of just over 100 feet, as well as explore the engine room, crew's quarters, and two cargo hold levels. Over the winter of 1986-87, however, strong currents in the channel caused part of the great sand bank which makes up Sand Point to shift nearly a hundred feet and drift over the MOORE, burying her to deck level and filling her lower decks with sand. In June, 1988, the Alger Underwater Preserve Committee organized the SMITH MOORE Project. Working with personnel from Continental Underwater, Incorporated of Edina, Minnesota, 37 divers from around the Midwest worked with airlifts for four days, literally vacuuming the sand off the deck and out of the engine trunk. Another dredging project the next year removed additional sand, keeping the stern deck clear. The point's shifting sands remain at deck level and continue to threaten the SMITH MOORE with eventual burial.

LOCATION: . . . . .46°27.33'N 86°37.06'W
DEPTH: . . . . .95 feet

REFERENCES:

Annual Report of the United States Life-Saving Service, 1895 (Washington, D.C.: Government Printing Office), pp. 100, 306.

Cleveland Plain Dealer, July 14, 15, 17, 19, 20, August 5, 1889.

Daily Mining Journal (Marquette, Michigan), July 15, 16, 19, August 1, 8, 1889.

Detroit Evening News, July 15, 30, August 1, September 6, 1889.

Detroit Free Press, July 13, 1889.

Mining Journal (Marquette, Michigan), May 1, July 10, September 18, 1880; June 30, 1881; September 8, 1883; July 4, September 6, December 6, 13, 1884; May 9, 1885; July 10, 24, 1886; July 20, August 10, 1889; August 26, 1966; October 21, 1967; June 8, 1988; May 26, 1992.

Sault Ste. Marie News, July 20, 27, August 3, 1889.

Wells, op. cit., pp. 18, 22.

CRUISER
August 20, 1891

Shipwreck can come in both the large and small variety. An example of the latter is the steam yacht CRUISER, lost off Chapel Beach. The CRUISER was brought to Munising from New York in 1891 by Mr. Ira F. Brainard, a wealthy tourist.

On Thursday August 20, Mr. Brainard and his party, consisting of his wife, son, two men friends and two women plus an engineer and local guide, left Grand Island for a day trip to the Pictured Rocks. Intending it to be a short excursion, they took only a picnic lunch. The trip had been planned earlier, but the Powell boys, local men knowledgeable of the challenges of the big lake, dissuaded them, believing the yacht was not suitable for such a trip. Eventually Brainard decided that he knew best and the trip was made.

As the Powells had foreseen, the party got caught in a heavy sea and decided to land at Chapel Beach, going ashore in small boats. The seas continued to build, and the yacht was unable to get out into the lake again. Abandoned, the yacht foundered at her anchorage. The pounding seas utterly destroyed the CRUISER, leaving only the machinery for potential salvage.

The shipwrecked tourists took shelter in a shallow cave near the beach. Although they built a roaring fire in front of the cave they still had a hard time staying warm in the unseasonably cold temperatures which accompanied the tempest. When it became apparent that no help would come to them through the continuing storm, the guide set off on foot for Munising. He reached town at about 2 p.m. on Saturday, and by 4 o'clock a rescue party had set out with a horse laden with provisions. The woods and swamps between Munising and the wreck site proved impassible for the horse, however, and the rescuers were forced to turn back that night.

Meanwhile, the fish tug FISHING QUEEN was trying to reach the stranded excursionists, but the high seas kept her from getting near Chapel Beach. Finally, on Sunday, her crew managed to float a small boat with some provisions to the party on shore - their first food in nearly three days. By Monday the seas had calmed enough that the FISHING QUEEN was able to rescue the Brainards and their guests, taking them off the beach in small boats. Doubtless they had a good tale to tell their friends back east about shipwreck on Lake Superior.

REFERENCES:

Daily Mining Journal (Marquette, Michigan), August 24, 25, 1891.

Detroit Evening News, August 25, 1891.

Mining Journal (Marquette, Michigan), August 29, 1891.

Wells, op. cit., p. 19.

MICHIGAN
September 21, 1893

Some tow barges were specially built for that purpose, while for others, the role of barge spelled the ignoble end to a long career on the lakes. One such vessel was the barge MICHIGAN.

The MICHIGAN was built in 1873 at Sandwich East, Ontario as a rail car ferry to run between Detroit, Michigan and Windsor, Ontario. She was a sidewheel steamer 265 feet long, 38.4 feet in beam and 14.2 in depth. After years of shuttling rail cars back and forth across the Detroit River, her engines and boilers were removed and she assumed the role of tow barge. Around 1890, she was being unloaded at Chicago when she broke in two and sank. Although she was raised and repaired, many vesselmen still felt she was structurally unsound.

On the night of September 21, 1893 the MICHIGAN was downbound on Lake Superior in tow of the steamer CITY OF NAPLES. After departing Marquette laden with iron ore, the steamer and tow experienced some heavy weather. As the MICHIGAN plunged through the growing seas, one of her arches broke and she began to leak uncontrollably. Captain Charles Olson signalled for the steamer to come about and take off the crew, which she did. At about midnight, when they were 20 miles east of Grand Island, the old barge plunged to the bottom 30 fathoms below. She was owned by the Gilchrist Company.

REFERENCES:

Alger County Republican (Munising, Michigan), September 29, 1893.

Daily Mining Journal (Marquette, Michigan), September 23, 1893.

Detroit Evening News, September 22, 1893.

George W. Hilton, *The Great Lakes Car Ferries* (Berkley, California: Howell-North, 1962), pp. 255-256.

Sault Ste. Marie News, September 23, 1893.

GEORGE
October 24, 1893

Another schooner lost at the Pictured Rocks was the GEORGE. Under Captain C.C. Roberts, she was headed for Marquette in tow of the steamer ITALIA with a cargo of 1,333 tons of coal consigned to the Pickands Company. At 6 p.m. on Monday the 23rd, when off Whitefish Point, the steamer dropped the tow line and the GEORGE sailed for Marquette under canvas with a fair south wind. By midnight she was past Au Sable Point Light and the wind began to shift and increase. When the schooner was in sight of the Grand Island North Light at 2:30 a.m. on the 24th, the wind veered sharply to the northwest and, in the words of Captain C.C. Roberts, "began to blow great guns."

The GEORGE altered course to run for the shelter of Grand Island. By 5 a.m. she was nearly in, when the gaff broke, then the foresail split! Minutes later the mizzen went to pieces. The GEORGE was left without enough sail to control her and was thrown to the mercy of the seas.

An hour and a half later the schooner was aground 100 feet off the rocks. Repeatedly she was struck with heavy seas. Since the towering cliffs prevented the crew from reaching shore directly, they lowered the yawl and rowed five miles through the tumultuous seas to safety at Grand Island.

Roberts remembered that it "was a cold, wet, hard pull." The nine occupants were happy indeed when the safety of the island was eventually reached. Local marine observers were pleased to notice that the schooner's cook was a buxom young Norwegian girl who was the envy of all who saw her. Doubtless she received the best of care.

The GEORGE was a broken wreck. The loss was cut somewhat when the tug C.E. BENHAM came down from Marquette towing the Marquette Life-Savers in their boat. Together they stripped the schooner of everything they could, an estimated $5,000 worth of gear. Owned by Miles Fox of Sandusky, she was a loss of $28,250.

The GEORGE was built as the GEORGE MURRAY in Manitowoc, Wisconsin in 1873. Measuring 202.8 feet in length, 34 feet in beam, 13.8 feet in depth and 790 gross tons, she was reputedly the largest ship of any kind built on Lake Michigan up to that time. Sold in 1880 to Chicago interests, she was renamed GEORGE in 1883.

Today the bare frames of the GEORGE can be found about 50 yards off the Pictured Rocks two miles northeast of Miners Castle, in approximately fifteen feet of water. On a clear day the outline of the wreck's remains is quite visible from the surface. Southwest of the hull, many small artifacts and pieces of wreckage can be found under and among the boulders close to shore.

COORDINATES: . . . . .46°30.96'N 86°31.25'W
DEPTH: . . . . .15 feet

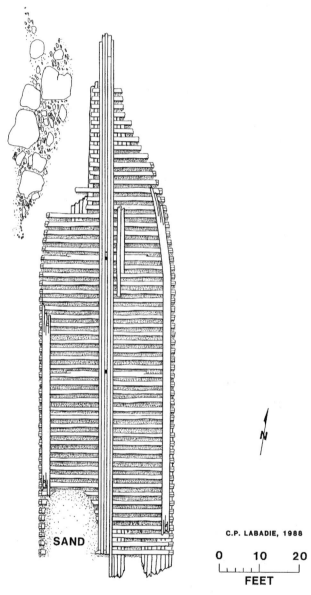

C.P. LABADIE, 1988

0   10   20

FEET

The hull of the GEORGE.

C. Patrick Labadie
Courtesy of the NPS Submerged
Cultural Resources Unit

REFERENCES:

Annual Report of the United States Life-Saving Service, 1894 (Washington, D.C.: Government Printing Office), pp. 109, 268.

Daily Mining Journal (Marquette, Michigan), October 26, 28, 1893.

Detroit Evening News, October 25, 26, 28, 1893.

Sault Ste. Marie News, October 28, November 4, 1893.

ELMA
September 29, 1895

D uring the last days of September 1895, early fall gales lashed the Great Lakes unmercifully. Everywhere vessels and lake port residents sought what refuge they could. In Manitowoc, on the west shore of Lake Michigan, the steamer WESTOVER barely made port with the schooner A.T. BLISS in tow, both badly damaged. The schooner had lost her entire deck load of lumber, as well as her mainmast and foremast. On Lake Huron, the tugs RELIANCE, MOCKINGBIRD and AVERY struggled mightily with a massive log raft. Finally, after a hard battle, they were able to bring it to shelter under Point Lookout near Tawas City. Lake Ontario was also roiled by the gales. Two schooners lay disabled and helpless under the Buffalo breakwall. The business of the famous iron port was at a complete standstill. At Port Colborne, Ontario, another schooner arrived badly mauled by powerful blasts. The schooner PAUL struggled into the harbor with her bulwarks, jib, mainsail and foresail carried away. Six miles from the breakwall, an unknown schooner was at anchor and flying distress signals. The severity of the storm prevented any immediate attempt at rescue.

It seems, however, that vessels on Lake Superior were receiving the worst of the battering by the storm gods. Upbound for Marquette, the steamer CHARLES J. KERSHAW and her two tows, the schooner MOONLIGHT and schooner-barge KENT, were proceeding well, in spite of the rolling gale. With the lights of Marquette flickering in the distance, disaster struck. A critical steam pipe burst on the KERSHAW, completely disabling her engine. Without the steamer's power, all three vessels were thrown to the mercy of the storm.

The MOONLIGHT and KENT eventually washed high up on a sand beach east of the city. Neither vessel was much damaged and both were eventually recovered, although the salvage effort required was long and expensive.

The KERSHAW was a different story. The screaming wind drove her hard on the Chocolay Reef, several hundred yards offshore from the schooners. Her crew was eventually rescued by the Marquette life-savers in one of the most spectacular operations ever conducted on the Great Lakes. In the KERSHAW rescue the life-savers truly earned their nickname of "storm warriors."

Lake conditions near the Pictured Rocks were just as fierce. The steamer WALLUDA, towing a whaleback barge, was mauled by the gale causing her to seek shelter behind Grand Island. The steamer had over five feet of water flooding her holds and her wheezing steam pumps could barely keep up.

The wooden schooner-barge ELMA, together with the schooner-barges CHESTER B. JONES and COMMODORE, had departed Pequaming, Michigan under the tow of the steamer P.H. BIRCKHEAD on Wednesday, September 25. All carried large loads of freshly milled lumber consigned to lower lake markets. The BIRCKHEAD was a powerful steamer with a reputation for large tows. On Thursday the BIRCKHEAD and her "string" took shelter in Marquette from the rough weather. When the lake quieted on Friday, the small fleet left in the evening to continue their long run down the lakes.

The calm experienced on leaving Marquette was short-lived. As they made their way to the Soo, the lake grew rougher and rougher. By the time they reached Whitefish Point on Saturday, a full lake storm was blowing. Desperate for shelter, the steamer turned to run under Whitefish Point for protection. Caught in the tenacious maw of the northwester, the tow lines parted and the steamer lost her schooners.

Three of the principals of the ELMA wreck: the schooner-barges COM-MODORE and CHESTER B. JONES and steamer P.H. BIRKENHEAD.
Hamilton Collection, Rutherford B. Hayes Library

The JONES was blown to within a mile and a half of the beach before her anchor caught, safely holding her off the breaking surf. Although surrounded by mountainous waves, the JONES held together throughout the terrible gale. For two long days, the local life-saving crew stood by on the beach opposite in case the schooner began to drift ashore, making it necessary to try to rescue the crew. On Monday evening the 30th, it looked like the end had come for the schooner, so the life-savers launched their trusty surfboat, battled through the heaving waves and pulled the crew off. Even in the somewhat moderated seas it was a difficult rescue. Several times the small surfboat capsized, but each time it was righted and the tough job continued. To the surprise of everyone, however, the JONES stayed together. Later the tug BOYNTON took the schooner and her crew through to Detroit.

After losing the tow line from the steamer, the COMMODORE was able to set her shortened sail rig and run for the safety of the Soo. Battered and leaking, she made it.

In spite of the mountainous seas, the BIRCKHEAD managed to pass a new tow line to the ELMA and started to make for shelter at Grand Island, 80 miles to the west. Near the Pictured Rocks, the tow line parted again. The slamming waves also broke the ELMA's steering gear, preventing any attempt to use her sails as the COMMODORE did. Helpless, the schooner was blown before the gale, rolling so badly in the trough of the waves that she literally jumped her masts out. Waterlogged and with her deck cargo long since washed off, she was only a drifting hulk, a ship and crew waiting to die!

Unable to help, the BIRCKHEAD ran for shelter at Grand Island, her captain hoping the schooner would wash up on the small sand beach near the Miners River. It was the only stretch of good beach in the whole area that wasn't rock. When the BIRCKHEAD reached Munising, her captain reported the accident and organized a rescue effort. Since the seas were too rough, he scouted the shore through the woods with George Prior, the East Channel lightkeeper. The only answer to their shouts was the crashing of the lake on the rocky shore. They would try again when the lake calmed, allowing them to use a boat to coast past the deadly cliffs.

Aboard the ELMA, things were desperate. The crew pumped continuously to try to keep her afloat as long as possible. Eventually the drifting hulk fetched up on a rock reef about 100 feet off Miners Castle. The master, Captain Thurston, quickly dropped his anchors which swung the ELMA off the reef and eased her pounding. The anchors held all day Sunday, but that night the chains parted and she drifted southward until she was driven full on the rock bottom about 100 feet from the base of the bluffs.

In an attempt to reach safety atop the towering cliffs, crewman George M. Johnson of Chicago tried to row the ELMA's small yawl to the cliff base with a line, but the crashing waves splintered the fragile boat against the rocks. Johnson, however, managed to scramble up the cliff face until he reached safety on a ledge 15 feet long and a bare three feet wide, but lost the all-important line during the climb.

Rudolf Yack of Mount Clemens, Michigan, another crewman and an excellent swimmer, volunteered to try to get a line to shore. Tying a rope around his waist he dove into the boiling water and struck boldly for the beach only to be dashed into the sharp rocks by the surf and killed. After numerous attempts, the crew stranded on the ELMA eventually succeeded in floating a line to Johnson. By the time this was accomplished it was too dark to try to bring the crew off. Throughout the long, cold storm-tossed night, the crew huddled on the ELMA, and Johnson paced his narrow ledge high on the rocks, firmly grasping the thin line. Under no circumstances could he drop it!

When daylight broke, he made his end fast to a nearby rock. One at a time, using the rope, all of the crew safely reached shore, including the captain's wife and three-year-old son. Mother and child were hauled over the deadly waves in a makeshift bosun's chair cobbled together from blankets. Using the same line, the entire crew managed to climb to a small ledge about 75 feet above the lake. There they built a fire and waited until Tuesday morning when the storm moderated.

The ELMA's crew was finally rescued through the persistent efforts of the lightkeeper. At daybreak on Tuesday, he and a local fisherman started to coast the rocky shore looking for survivors or wreckage. A little after 8 a.m. they sighted the cold and hungry crew. Keeper Prior in turn signaled the BIRCKHEAD which was three miles out and on her way down to the Soo. The steamer happily returned and took the survivors aboard.

The ELMA was later examined for the underwriters by Captain Martin Daniels of Marquette. He reported that as a result of the storm beating, her hull was broken and shattered, and she was rapidly going to pieces. Captain Daniels was, however, able to salvage a small amount of her lumber cargo.

In examining the wreck, Daniels saw the rope the crew used to climb the cliffs still dangling down from the rocks. Daniels reported, "the man who went up there with that line must have been a good one." He and some of his crew tried in vain to make the same climb.

Built in 1873 in Marine City, Michigan, as a three-masted tow barge, the ELMA was a loss of $9,000. Unfortunately she carried little insurance. Her dimensions were 165.2 feet in length, 30 feet in beam, 11 feet in depth and 900.68 gross tons.

During a sidescan sonar survey of the Alger Underwater Preserve in the early 1980's, an anchor believed to belong to the ELMA was found near Miners Castle. The anchor lies in 43 feet of water, and probably marks the crew's last-ditch effort to keep the ELMA from piling onto the rocks. The anchor is still set, and the chain still trails off from it toward the cliffs, though buried in sand. Although no hull wreckage has been found that can be positively identified as belonging to the ELMA, some marine historians believe that some of the broken schooner pieces littering the shallows north of Sand Point may be hers.

COORDINATES: . . . . .46°29.55'N 86°33.74'W (Anchor)
DEPTH: . . . . .43 feet (Anchor)

REFERENCES:

Annual Report of the United States Life-Saving Service, 1896 (Washington, D.C.: Government Printing Office), pp. 88, 331.

Cleveland Plain Dealer, September 30, October 1, 2, 1895.

Daily Mining Journal (Marquette, Michigan), October 1, 2, 5, 11, 17, 1895.

Detroit Evening News, October 1, 2, 9, 1895.

Detroit Free Press, October 2, 1895.

Detroit Tribune, October 2, 1895.

Mining Journal (Marquette, Michigan), October 12, 1895.

Sault Ste. Marie News, October 12, 1895.

MICHAEL GROH
November 22, 1895

The old steam-barge MICHAEL GROH, under the command of Captain Michael Groh, was downbound from Marquette with a cargo of 325,000 board feet of lumber when she ran into high winds and heavy seas off Grand Island. The GROH ran for shelter, but before she could gain the lee of the island, a wave unshipped her rudder and she was blown helplessly before the storm. Rolling in the trough, she shipped seas over her sides until the engineroom crew were working knee-deep in water. They kept the steam up and the engine running in a vain attempt to reach shelter. At 7:25 Friday morning, the steamer was blown into the Pictured Rocks where she grounded on a rock reef just offshore, near the site where the ELMA had wrecked just two months earlier. Quickly she stove in her hull and sank up to her decks. The dozen crew took to the boats and escaped to safety ashore.

Rapid work by Captain John H. Gillett of Marquette, using the tug GILLETT and Captain Martin Daniels with his schooner the CRISS GROVER, managed to save 140,000 feet of the lumber cargo. However, the GROH was in a bad position and it was apparent that the next storm would destroy her. Still, there was hope that the vessel could be pulled free and the powerful Inman tug W.B. CASTLE was telegraphed for. Before she arrived, the feared storm arrived on November 30 and pounded the GROH to pieces, a loss of $9,000. The following summer, the Whitney Brothers of Duluth salvaged the engine, boiler and running gear, which they put into a new tug they were building. The original lumber cargo, consigned to the Cleveland Sawmill and Lumber Company, was valued at $8,900.

The schooner CRISS GROVER was a salvage veteran, having just returned from Isle Royale where she had participated in the recovery of the wrecked steamer CENTURIAN and her cargo. The GROVER herself was later lost to shipwreck, going ashore near Split Rock on Superior's North Shore in 1899.

The MICHAEL GROH was built in Cleveland by Quayle and Martin in 1867 with dimensions of 120.4 feet in length, 23.8 feet in beam, 8.6 feet in depth and 174.15 gross tons. During the winter of 1881-82, she was rebuilt in Muskegon, adding 20 feet to her length, two to her beam and increasing the gross tonnage to 289.1. The steamer ran in the lumber trade for nearly three decades, with occasional work as a wrecking tug.

At least two pieces of the GROH's hull can be seen in the shallow waters north of Sand Point. One section, a triangular piece about 15 feet long and 14 feet wide, comprises the sternmost part of her lower hull, including her engine mounting beds. This piece lies in about 10 feet of water less than a quarter mile off shore. A second, larger piece about a quarter mile away measures 104 feet long and about 24 feet wide. The massive keelsons and frames make up most of the steamer's bottom. Both pieces of the MICHAEL GROH can be elusive, as they are subject to Sand Point's shifting sands and may be covered or exposed according to the lake's whims.

COORDINATES: . . . . . .46°27.74'N 86°35.59'W (Engine bed)
46°27.73'N 86°35.86'W (Hull)
DEPTH: . . . . .10-12 feet

REFERERENCES:

Alger County Republican (Munising, Michigan), August 28, September 18, 1896.

Daily Mining Journal (Marquette, Michigan), November 26, 29, December 2, 1895.

Detroit Evening News, November 23, 25, 29, 1895.

Detroit Free Press, November 22, 1895.

Detroit Tribune, December 23, 1867.

Mining Journal (Marquette, Marquette), November 23, 30, December 7, 1895.

Sault Ste. Marie News, November 30, 1895.

Wells, op. cit., p. 24.

MANHATTAN
October 26, 1903

The Gilchrist steamer MANHATTAN, downbound from Duluth for Buffalo with a cargo of grain, was forced by northerly gales to shelter behind Grand Island. After the weather moderated late on the night of October 25th, the MANHATTAN started down the east channel for the open lake. About midnight, when she was opposite the East Channel Light, her steering chain broke, causing her to veer off course and smash into a reef just off the channel. The impact was strong enough to knock over chairs, dishes, tools and other loose items, among which was a burning kerosene lantern in the after cabin. The resulting fire caught quickly and soon was roaring out of control.

The crew was taken off by the Powell and Mitchell tug WARD. The wooden steamer burned to the water's edge, and together with her cargo of 76,000 bushels of wheat, was a total loss. The MANHATTAN was insured for $50,000 and the cargo for $65,000.

The 1,545-ton MANHATTAN, a comparatively modern and staunch vessel, was built by the Detroit Dry Dock Company in Detroit in 1887 for the Inter Ocean Transportation Company of Milwaukee. Measuring 252.4 feet by 38 feet by 19 feet, she had two decks and three masts. Iron straps crisscrossed her hull under her planking to provide additional strength. Innovative for her time, she had a steel boiler house, steam pumps and windlass, and electric lights. The Inter Ocean Company operated a fleet of wooden steamers and specialized in bulk cargos of grain, salt and iron ore. Hauling ore from Escanaba to Cleveland was a common run. The company gradually upgraded its fleet to steel vessels and in 1898 sold the MANHATTAN and three other wooden steamers to the J.C. Gilchrist fleet for $70,000. The MANHATTAN was the seventh vessel of the Gilchrist fleet lost during the 1903 season. The others were the MOONLIGHT, WAVERLY, SWAIN, CRAIG, A.A. PARKER, and MARQUETTE. All were wooden vessels and, oddly for the Gilchrist Company which made a

The wooden steamer MANHATTAN.
HAMILTON COLLECTION, RUTHERFORD B. HAYES LIBRARY

frequent practice of saving money by not insuring their vessels, all were insured during the 1903 season.

The wreck of the MANHATTAN was sold at auction in 1905 for $1600. Apparently her new owners salvaged her engine, boilers, and the coal from her bunkers, but the burned-out hulk itself was too difficult to move without great effort and expense. The wreck was just on the west edge of the channel and posed a danger to navigation. In 1910 the federal government contracted with Thomas Durocher of Sault Ste. Marie, Michigan to remove the wreck for the sum of $1,900. His method seems to have been to first recover any salvageable material, mostly iron and steel, then knock the hull down.

Due to the actions of the salvagers, as well as the destructive forces of the lake's wind and ice, the remains of the MANHATTAN are widely spread along the west side of the east channel. The shallowest sections, in about 15 feet of water, can often be seen from the surface.

The MANHATTAN on the morning after. Smoke still curls up from the forward end of the steamer.

MARQUETTE MARITIME MUSEUM

Divers can visit a large portion of the steamer's hull framing, including massive timbers and the distinctive iron strapping, in about 25 feet. The vessel's enormous rudder, with its depth markings still visible, lies nearby, along with some of the deck fittings and machinery. Additional portions of the hull can be found farther out in the channel in depths down to 40 feet.

    COORDINATES: . . . . .46°27.98'N 86°36.62'W
    DEPTH: . . . . .15-40 feet

REFERENCES:

Annual Report, Lake Carriers Association, 1911.

Daily Mining Journal (Marquette, Michigan), October 28, 29, November 17, 1903; June 5, 1905.

Detroit Evening News, October 27, 28, 1903; June 5, 1905; July 10, 1910.

Duluth Herald, July 30, 1910.

Duluth News-Tribune, October 28, 1903.

Mining Journal (Marquette, Michigan), October 31, November 21, 1903.

Wells, op. cit., p. 32.

SITKA
October 4, 1904

Another victim of the treacherous Au Sable Reef was the wooden steamer SITKA. She was en route from Marquette to Toledo with a cargo of iron ore when she wandered south of her course and at 6 p.m. on October 4, 1904, ran hard on the reef. The SITKA found herself out two feet forward, sitting on a rock ledge with only twelve feet of water over it about a mile offshore. The day of the accident was dark and misty, but there was no wind and no sea running, thus the reason for the stranding isn't clear.

The 272-foot wooden steamer SITKA.   C. PATRICK LABADIE

The Grand Marais Life-Saving Station first learned of the SITKA's plight from the coastal steamer HUNTER at 7:30 p.m. The HUNTER was returning to Grand Marais from Munising and signaled the news of the wreck when she came abreast of the station. Rounding up his crew, keeper Benjamin Trudell launched his Beebe-McLellan surfboat and pulled for the wreck, arriving about 11:20 p.m., covering the nine miles in three hours. The SITKA was discovered to be leaking badly but the crew wasn't ready to abandon her. The captain, F. E. Johnson, however, asked Trudell to take several messages back to Grand Marais requesting tugs from the Soo to pull his vessel free. Instead of rowing back to port, Trudell landed one man at Au Sable Light and sent him back overland with the dispatches.

The life-savers remained on the beach at the lighthouse and kept a close watch on the weather. By 5 a.m. the next morning the wind and the sea had increased noticeably. Suspecting a change of heart, the life-savers pulled out to the steamer and found the crew was now ready to abandon her. Using the SITKA's two yawls and the surfboat, all seventeen of the crew plus all their baggage were safely landed on the sand beach at the foot of the lighthouse.

The SITKA's crew then departed overland for Grand Marais, leaving their bags at the lighthouse. The increasing seas and wind, however, weather-bound the life-savers at the light until 1 p.m. on the 9th. From the beach they watched as the gale and high seas methodically destroyed the steamer. First the deckhouses were swept away. Then her rudder broke loose. Finally the ship broke aft of the main mast. The storm-bound life-savers were furnished forty meals by lightkeeper Otto Bufe at a charge of 25 cents each. Reimbursement was made though proper channels upon presentation of appropriate forms. Government red tape existed even 75 years ago.

On their way back to Grand Marais, the life-savers stopped at the wreck and salvaged her compasses and other valuable navigation instruments.

The following day, at the request of F.E. Johnson, the master of the SITKA, and Captain Weeks, the commodore of the Gilchrist Fleet, the crew in their surfboat was towed out to the wreck behind the tug SCHENCK and assisted in stripping her of some remaining salvageable items. The SITKA was valued at $45,000 and the cargo at $8,225, making her a total loss of $53,225. No insurance was carried on the vessel. This was a common practice for the Gilchrist Company, especially at the end of the season when rates were very high.

In the fall of 1906, Captain Davidson of Grand Marais salvaged the wreck's boilers by floating them and towing them to Grand Marais Harbor. The following year he sold them to a chemical plant in Detroit.

The SITKA was built in West Bay City by the F.W. Wheeler Company in 1887 for the Wilson Transportation Company of Cleveland. During this period the Wilson Company was very important in Great Lakes sailing. In 1887 alone, the company built three steamers and two big schooner-barges.

The SITKA measured 272.5 feet in length, 40.5 feet in beam, 19.4 feet in depth and 1,740 gross tons. A triple expansion Frontier Iron Works steam engine provided 800 horsepower at 85 revolutions per minute. Her wood hull was heavily reinforced with steel strapping and she had a specially strengthened bow. Building cost was estimated at $110,000.

When she slid down her launch ways, the steamer was virtually complete and ready to go, because four days later she was upbound for Two Harbors for ore. As was common during the times, she usually towed a barge. To increase her speed and power, she was reboiled in 1890, her original water tube units being replaced with scotch boilers.

In 1903 the SITKA was sold to the Gilchrist Transportation Company. The Wilson fleet was buying new steel ships and even though she was well maintained, wood hulls had to go.

Ironically, the HUNTER, the small coastal steamer that signaled the news of the SITKA's loss, was destroyed by fire the same day, while lying at the Booth dock in Grand Marais.

The SITKA had earlier brushes with shipwreck. In May 1893, she was aground on Kettle Point Reef, Lake Huron. After lightering, patching and pumping, she slid off the reef. In October that same year, while steaming off Whitefish Point, she picked up a yawl containing five half-dead sailors from the schooner ANNIE SHERWOOD. Thinking their ship was on the way down as the result of being smashed by a roaring gale, the men had abandoned ship. The schooner was later discovered battered and broken on the Canadian shore near Otter Head.

Today miscellaneous pieces of the SITKA litter the Au Sable Reef area. Nearly the whole bottom of her hull, measuring approximately 198 feet by 40 feet, can still be found in the surf line about one half mile west of the Au Sable Light. Smaller pieces of her hull can be found in the shallows closer to the light. Off the west side of the reef, divers have reported a large field of wreckage including the stern section of the hull in 25 feet of water.

REFERENCES:

Annual Report of the United States Life-Saving Service, 1905 (Washington, D.C.: Government Printing Office), pp. 95, 296-297.

Harvey Childs Beeson, *Beeson's Inland Marine Directory 1905,* (Chicago: Harvey C. Beeson, 1905), p. 122

Chicago Tribune, May 3, 1893.

Daily Mining Journal (Marquette, Michigan), October 6, 7, 1904; April 7, 1905; June 24, August 9, 1907.

Detroit Evening News, October 5, 6, 7, 8, 1904; August 27, 1906.

Duluth News-Tribune, October 5, 25, 1904.

Telegram, Grand Marais Life-Saving Station to Life-Saving Station, Washington, D.C., October 4, 1904, National Archives, Record Group 26.

Wreck Report, Steamer SITKA, October 4, 1904, National Archives, Record Group 26.

ALTA
October 19, 1905

A t 11 a.m. on Friday, October 20, the steamer MYER slowly worked her way in past the Marquette harbor breakwater. A heavy sea was still running from a two-day-old lake blow and the breakwater was being constantly inundated with rolling gray seas. The steamer had a decided list to port and her deck load of lumber showed the evidence of having been battered by the powerful waves. The MYER had earlier attempted to shelter in Grand Island Harbor but when she reached the approaches a blinding blizzard totally obscured the channel. For safety her captain ran her to Marquette.

The captain also reported that she had lost her two tows, the 178-foot, 593-ton schooner-barge OLGA and the 198-foot 935-ton schooner-barge ALTA, during the height of the storm the past Thursday. All three vessels were downbound from Duluth with lumber for Tonawanda, New York, when they were caught by the storm off Grand Marais. The MYER attempted to reach shelter with his charges in Grand Marais harbor, but at 8 p.m. he lost them both when their tow lines snapped.

Both the ALTA and the OLGA were at the mercy of the storm and were punished terribly. The grasping seas soon swept off their deck loads of lumber and the severe tossing and pitching caused the masts to be literally thrown out of the hulls by the tremendous wave action. The ALTA also had her cabins swept off, while the OLGA lost her rudder.

Within two hours the ALTA was driven high on a Grand Island shoal, near Trout Bay. Her crew of six men and one woman (the cook) were rescued by small boats from Grand Island. All were reported to be utterly exhausted and had lost all their possessions in the wreck.

The OLGA was far more lucky. Her anchors caught just in the nick of time and her chains held her safely off the deadly Pictured Rocks. Captain A.C. Loudin was the hero of the ship when he dove into the wild lake to rescue one of his crewmen. The beleaguered and sorely

The schooner-barge ALTA.   C. PATRICK LABADIE

tried crew stayed aboard until Saturday morning when they launched their yawl and rowed to safety. The OLGA was later recovered and after repairs, returned to service.

The ALTA, however, was in a much more precarious position. When the storm abated, Captain Andrew Scott inspected his vessel and found her with her stern high on the rocks a mere 25 feet from shore and her bow sunk in 18 feet of water. The Reid Wrecking Company bought the wrecked schooner and sent the wrecking tug OTTAWA to try to raise her. Reid's diver, however, discovered that a sharp rock had pierced her hull and held her in place on the sloping bottom. The famous salvager Captain Tom Reid had to be satisfied with recovering the lumber from her hold. Much of the deck loads from the two schooner-barges had washed ashore between Miners River and Mosquito River and was salvaged by enterprising local men who sold it back to Reid. Storms and ice that winter battered the ALTA into kindling.

The OLGA didn't last much longer. On November 26, 1905 she broke loose from the MYER during a Lake Huron gale. When it looked like she would sink, the crew safely abandoned her. However, she drifted about for several days, eventually coming ashore north of Goderich, Ontario where she was pounded to pieces by the waves.

The ALTA was launched in April 1884 by Thomas F. Murphy at Cleveland, under sub-contract to the F.B. Wheeler yard of West Bay City. Originally built as a three-masted schooner, she was later cut down to a schooner-barge. Her dimensions were 198 feet in length, 37.4 feet in beam and 15.7 feet in depth. She was a loss of $10,000.

REFERENCES:

Daily Mining Journal (Marquette, Michigan), October 21, 23, November 29, December 13, 1905.

Detroit Evening News, October 21, 22, November 5, 1905.

Duluth New-Tribune, October 22, 30, November 22, 23, 1905.

David D. Swayze, Ralph K. Roberts, and Donald Comtois, *Vessels Built on the Saginaw,* Volume 1 (Bay City, Michigan: Saginaw River Marine Historical Society, 1993), p. 2.

Richard J. Wright, *Freshwater Whales, A History of the American Ship Building Company and its Predecessors* (Kent State University Press, 1971). pp. 116.

CULLIGAN
September 27, 1912

Four hours after leaving Marquette with a cargo of 2,100 tons of iron ore, the 263-foot, 1,748-ton wooden steamer CULLIGAN was discovered to be leaking badly. Although she had been taking on water during her last two trips, it had never seemed serious and had always been within her pump's capability. Now, however, there was no question that it had reached an alarming level. Accordingly her master, Captain Henry Richardson, headed her for Grand Island where he intended to ground her on a shallow bar.

At 9:30 a.m. on the 27th, when it became apparent they were not going to make it, the captain and crew abandoned the CULLIGAN in her two lifeboats. The seas were rough and it was difficult to make headway under oar power alone, so the crew in one of the boats jury-rigged a sail out of a tablecloth, an oar and a pikepole. With her boiler fires out due to the rising water, the steamer drifted until about 2:30

At 2:30 p.m. September 27, 1912, the CULLIGAN dove for the bottom. The wreck is still undiscovered.

KEN E. THRO

p.m. when she gave up the ghost and plunged to the bottom. As inevitably occurs when a wooden steamer sounds, her pilothouse broke off and came bobbing to the surface. The crew was later rescued by the fish tug COLUMBIA and taken back to Marquette.

The CULLIGAN was an old boat, having been built at West Bay City, Michigan by James Davidson in 1883. Originally named the GEORGE T. HOPE, she was renamed the CULLIGAN in 1907. The owner at the time of the sinking was John J. Boland of the Boland & Cornelius steamboat fleet. The CULLIGAN was a loss of $25,000.

REFERENCES:

Captain Edward Carus, *"100 Years of Disasters on the Great Lakes."* Unpublished Manuscript, 1931.

Daily Mining Journal (Marquette, Michigan), September 28, 30, 1912.

Detroit Evening News, September 28, 1912.

Detroit Free Press, September 28, 1912

Wells, op. cit., p. 48.

SOUTH SHORE
November 24, 1912

The small wooden steamer SOUTH SHORE was steaming west from the Soo bound for Grand Marais on November 23 when she was engulfed in a strong northeast gale accompanied by blinding snow squalls. The storm, reputed to be the worst in fifteen years, broke up log booms in sheltered Munising Bay and also toppled a pile driver off a scow and into the water. Since the huge seas prevented any attempt to enter the dangerous Grand Marais pierhead, the steamer's master, Ora Endress, a very experienced sailor, elected to try to ride out the gale in the open lake.

Throughout the long wild night the small SOUTH SHORE battled the gale and in return was badly battered. Keeping her bow into the combers, Endress kept slowing working his way northeast toward Caribou Island, 45 miles distant. By midnight, when he was about 25 miles northeast of Grand Marais, her seams had opened and she was leaking badly. Part of her cabin had gone overboard and her wheelhouse was partially destroyed. Windows were smashed in and thick ice coated everything. Most important of all, the rising water in her hold had reached her boiler fires and extinguished them! Without power, she rolled into the deadly trough and was driven helplessly before the gale. Desperately, crew and passengers worked her hand pumps to keep her afloat. The SOUTH SHORE was nothing more than a waterlogged wreck.

Shortly after 8 a.m., the Grand Marais life-savers' lookout spotted the steamer about ten miles out. Although the SOUTH SHORE wasn't flying distress signals, Captain Trudell, the legendary keeper of the Grand Marais station, bravely led his crew out into the storm-swept lake in their new power lifeboat, nicknamed AUDACITY. When they reached the nearly-awash steamer they attempted to save her by dumping cargo, working her pumps and trying to rebuild her boiler fires, but when it became apparent that their efforts were futile, the life-savers took off the four passengers and the ten-man crew. Later the abandoned steamer drifted to within 100 yards of the shore, eventually sinking in twelve feet of water about two miles east of Au Sable Point.

Lying in such an exposed positon, the SOUTH SHORE went to pieces quickly after sinking. Little identifiable wreckage from the steamer can be found today. The SOUTH SHORE's boiler lies in shallow water offshore from the Grand Sable Dunes, and can often be seen from the top of the dunes. What are probably pieces of her hull lie in shallow water near the Log Slide, but these are often totally buried in sand.

The SOUTH SHORE was a loss of about $8,000. Some small items including two small yawls, a liferaft, several cork jackets and some cargo, totalling about $200 in value were later recovered from the wreck.

The small steamer SOUTH SHORE.

MARQUETTE MARITIME MUSEUM

The heroic work by the Grand Marais life-savers earned them a tribute from long-time General Superintendent Sumner I. Kimball, who praised them as "a bully boat and a bully crew."

The SOUTH SHORE started life in 1899 as the tug ROBERT E. BURKE. Built in Manitowoc, Wisconsin by Burger for the Independent Tug Line of Chicago, she was a very typical harbor tug. Her measurements were 84.3 feet in length, 20.7 feet in beam, 6.3 feet in depth and 73 gross tons. She was employed in the harbor towing trade as well as for excursion trips from the Chicago River to Jackson and Lincoln Parks. While in winter layup at Muskegon in 1901 the tug suffered a major fire, losing all her upper works as well as damaging her hull.

Electing not to repair her, the owners sold the tug to the Graham and Morton Company who rebuilt the BURKE into a passenger steamer, giving her two open decks for excursionists as well as a small interior cabin on the lower deck. She again cruised the Chicago lake front route. Less than six months later, the BURKE was again sold, this time to the Howard Transportation Company of Chicago. During this period she continued sailing the Chicago area and carried freight between the city and Lockport, Illinois, via the canals. In 1908 her name was changed to SOUTH SHORE.

Emil G. Endress of Sault Ste. Marie, Michigan purchased her in the spring of 1909 and used her to carry passengers and freight between various ports on the east end of the lake as far west as Marquette. To better accommodate Superior's cold weather, her open lower deck was closed in and a passenger cabin was built on the upper deck. Included in her stops were the string of isolated Lake Superior life-saving stations at Vermilion Point, Crisp's Point, Two-Hearted River, Deer Park and Grand Marais as well as the lighthouses at Whitefish Point and Au Sable. The SOUTH SHORE was a critical link for many of the small settlements and her loss was sorely felt. The 75 tons of freight she carried on her last trip were in some instances supplies intended to last out the long winter for many people.

REFERENCES:

Annual Report of the United States Life-Saving Service, 1912 (Washington, D.C.: Government Printing Office), pp. 172, 99, 124.

Daily Mining Journal (Marquette, Michigan), November 26, 27, 29, December 2, 14, 1912.

Detroit Evening News, November 25, December 13, 1912.

Labadie, op. cit., pp. 138-141.

Munising News, November 29, 1912.

Port Huron Daily Times, December 23, 1901.

Wells, op. cit., p. 49.

GALE STAPLES
October 1, 1918

The old wooden steamer GALE STAPLES under Captain Graham, loaded with coal, was upbound for Port Arthur when a strong north gale blew her hard onto Au Sable Reef, striking about three quarters of a mile off shore and abreast of the Au Sable Point Lighthouse. The stranded steamer was spotted by the lookout at the Grand Marais Coast Guard Station at 4 p.m. Although the keeper in charge of the station, Benjamin Trudell, was absent on liberty, the number one surfman A.E. Kristofferson quickly called all hands and launched the power lifeboat. The crew reached the stranded steamer, which was about eight miles west of the station, at about 5 p.m. (Ironically, Trudell would also be absent on leave the following year when his crew, again led by Kristofferson, would rescue the crew of the wooden steamer H.B. RUNNELS, wrecked just west of the Grand Marais harbor entrance on November 14, 1919. The rescue was so daring, the members of the Coast Guard crew plus several volunteers each received a gold life-saving medal.

The GALE STAPLES was another victim of Au Sable Reef.
KEN E. THRO

Since there was still hope of saving the steamer, the Coast Guard returned to Grand Marais without removing the crew, but instead sent telegrams to the Soo on their behalf calling for tugs and to the owners advising them of their vessel's plight. Later the Coast Guard returned to the steamer and stood by throughout the night.

At 8 a.m. on October 2, the Coast Guard returned to the station from the GALE STAPLES bringing with them one sailor and the two women cooks. All three were furnished with a hot dinner at the station. The Coast Guard crew went back to the steamer at 9:30 a.m. to deliver a reply to the earlier telegram, only to return to the station again shortly after 2 p.m. with four more sailors. At the request of the captain, the members of the STAPLES's crew already ashore were taken to a local hotel. When the Coast Guard crew returned to the steamer at 5 p.m., the wind had increased significantly and angry seas were breaking aboard. Since there was danger of the ship breaking up, the Coast Guard took the captain and the ten remaining sailors off and delivered them to the dock opposite the hotel.

When the Grand Marais Coast Guard Station keeper, Benjamin Trudell, arrived back at his post at 11 p.m. he found a beehive of efficient activity. As usual, the Coast Guardsmen were performing their difficult tasks like clockwork.

When the weather moderated on the 3rd, the Coast Guard returned the STAPLES's captain and ten of his crew to the steamer. Captain Graham was still optimistic about getting his ship off the reef. Keeper Trudell, however, had doubts. Wisely he canceled any liberty for his crew and set them to preparing their equipment for further use. If a norther blew up, as they were apt to at Au Sable, they would have to pluck the crew off quickly!

For the next three days the weather remained reasonably good and the Coast Guardsmen were employed in carrying telegrams out to the steamer advising her master of progress in sending the requested tugs. But sitting on a Lake Superior reef isn't good for a ship under any circumstances and even moderate waves can do heavy damage. The waves continued to batter the GALE STAPLES. On October 6, the Au

Sable lightkeeper noted in his journal that her upper cabin was gone and the ship appeared to have broken forward of the cabin.

On the 7th, Captain F.D. Root, with the Great Lakes Towing Company tug ILLINOIS and the lighter RELIANCE, arrived on the scene and the Coast Guard crew piloted them over the treacherous reef to the STAPLES. The Coast Guard also transported Captain A.C. Hansen, the Marine Insurance Agent, out to the wreck so he could personally assess the situation. After recovering about 1600 tons of the coal cargo, the salvors abandoned the steamer as hopeless and a loss of $75,000. She eventually broke up completely.

The reef where the GALE STAPLES wrecked is a broad, smooth expanse of sandstone reaching a mile out into the lake, exposed to Superior's fury from all directions. Three quarters of a century of storms and ice have reduced the STAPLES to a scattered field of wreckage. The reef is strewn with the remnants of a wooden steamer - boilers, propeller, rudder, anchor, capstan, valves, tools, miscellaneous machine parts, and thousands of fasteners, large and small.

The most prominent features on the reef are the GALE STAPLES's two massive Scotch boilers lying 250 feet apart in 15 feet of water and easily visible from the surface. The eastern boiler sits by itself near the margin of the reef, while the western one is surrounded by a field of wreckage. Lying next to the west boiler is one of the steamer's 1500-pound Trotman folding-stock anchors. About 100 feet north is the propeller, with three of its four blades broken off. The propeller is still attached to its shaft, which in turn remains in place in its tube through the stern deadwood. East of the propeller lie the enormous iron-sheathed wooden rudder and its iron tiller.

South of the boilers, a wide trail of debris leads in toward shore. The wreckage is thickest just inshore from the west boiler, where divers can find small pieces of hardware, fasteners, engine parts, and deck equipment, including one of the steamer's capstans. Occasional artifacts can be found all the way in to the shoreline half a mile away, where several pieces of the STAPLES's wooden hull can be found half buried in the sand at the surf line. Two small sections can be seen about

900 feet west of the Au Sable Light, right alongside a larger piece of the SITKA. A third piece of the STAPLES is located 1000 feet east of the light. The majority of the hull, however, has not been located. It may well lie in the deeper water off the east side of the reef, pushed there by winter's ice and the prevailing westerly winds.

The bulk freighter GALE STAPLES was built as the W.B. MORELY in 1888 at Marine City by Morely and Hill. Her dimensions were 295 feet in length, 42 feet in beam, 24 feet in depth and 1,846.59 gross tons. At the time of launching, the local paper referred to her as a "marine monster." With a cargo capacity of 2,650 tons, she had two decks and four masts. Diagonal steel straps reinforced her heavy oak framing. After launching the hull was towed to Detroit for the installation of her engine, a powerful 1,150 horsepower triple expansion unit built by the Detroit Dry Dock Engine Works. She was valued at $130,000.

During her first season she ran on the Lake Michigan - Buffalo grain route. The next year she was sold to the Corrigan Fleet of Cleveland and her named changed to CALEDONIA. During this period she frequently towed a barge and ran from the lower lakes to Two Harbors or Ashland for ore.

In 1900 she was rebuilt in Duluth, coming out with only one mast, new decking, a water ballast system and steam pumps. Historian C. Patrick Labadie noted that the rebuilding many have been done to raise the ship's insurance classification, thus saving the owners considerable money in reduced premiums. Insurance rates were determined by the classification or "rating" of the vessel. Wooden ships with steel strapping were eligible for an "A-1" rating for not more than ten years after construction. Rebuilding was required to maintain the high rating.

As the Corrigan fleet moved into steel vessels, it sold most of its wooden hulls. In 1907 they removed the CALEDONIA's engine and put it into the steel barge POLYNESIA, converting her into a steamer. The CALEDONIA's hull was then sold to John J. Boland of Buffalo, who re-powered her with the engine from the steamer KITTIE M. FORBES. The new powerplant was a two cylinder engine dating from

1883 and, at 500 horsepower, had less than half the power of the old one. Boland ran the steamer primarily in the coal and salt trade.

In 1912 she was sold to the Great Lakes Engineering Works, who in turn chartered her out for the 1913, 1914 and 1915 seasons. The following year she was sold to the Davidson and Smith Elevator Company of Port Arthur and renamed the GALE STAPLES. She sailed only two years under her new name before meeting her fate on Lake Superior.

COORDINATES: . . . . .46°40.80'N 86°09.09'W
DEPTH: . . . . .20 feet

REFERENCES:

Detroit Free Press, October 23, 1888.

Labadie, op. cit., pp. 121-132.

Log of Coast Guard Station at Grand Marais, Michigan. October 1-8, 1918. National Archives, Record Group 26.

Daily Mining Journal (Marquette, Michigan), August 21, 1888.

Port Huron Daily Times, January 4, 1889.

WOOD ISLAND
September 9, 1922

One of the few fire losses in the Pictured Rocks areas was that of the small 45-foot wooden tug WOOD ISLAND, lost on the night of September 9, 1922. The tug was en route from Munising to the mouth of the Whitefish River with an empty log boom when the accident happened. At 10 p.m. an engine backfired through the carburetor, spraying burning gasoline throughout the interior of the cabin. It was thought that water in the gas caused the actual backfire. Although Captain Angus Steinoff and his two-man crew tried to extinguish the fire, they were not successful.

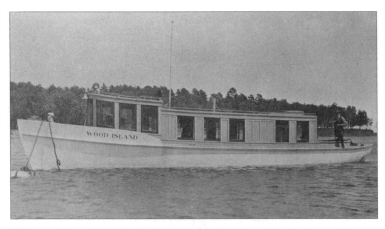

The small tug WOOD ISLAND burned and sank after a carburetor backfired. MARQUETTE CO. HISTORICAL SOCIETY

The crew stayed aboard until the flames threatened the rear gas tank; then they abandoned her in the yawl. Minutes later the tank exploded. A while later the forward tank blew with a roar and its flash illuminated the lake for hundreds of yards. At 10:15 p.m. the WOOD ISLAND sank. Captain Steinoff estimated the wreck was about one and a half miles off Five Mile Point in approximately 60 feet of water.

The crew was rescued by the tug GRAND ISLAND, owned by the Cleveland Cliffs Iron Company (CCI). The WOOD ISLAND had planned to meet the GRAND ISLAND at 4 a.m. in Shelter Bay.

It is interesting to note that such accidents today to gas powered boats are relatively uncommon as the result of Coast Guard regulations requiring the use of flame arresters on carburetors.

The WOOD ISLAND was built by the Racine Boat Company in 1907 for Marcus A. Doty who used her in a passenger service between Munising, Grand Island, and the Pictured Rocks. In 1917 she was purchased by CCI. When the tug joined the CCI fleet, she was modified, having a double tow post built in the stern and repowered with twin 40 horsepower Doman engines. CCI used her to tow log rafts from Grand Island to the company sawmill, as well as to assist other company vessels in passenger service between Grand Island and Munising.

REFERENCE:

Daily Mining Journal (Marquette, Michigan), September 12, 13, 1922.

HERMAN H. HETTLER
November 23, 1926

The 36 year old wooden steamer HERMAN H. HETTLER was seeking shelter in Munising Harbor from a fall gale when a reported compass variation caused her to veer off course and slam into the rock reef off Trout Point, at the north end of the east channel. The HETTLER, under Captain John M. Johnson, was en route from Ludington, Michigan to Duluth with a cargo of 1,100 tons of bulk table salt. The accident happened about 8:30 p.m. while visibility was restricted by heavy snow squalls.

The HERMAN H. HETTLER heavily laden with a deck load of barrelled cargo.   KEN E. THRO

The HETTLER on the reef!   Edward Pusick

The force of the grounding was so severe that it ran the steamer on the rocks up to her third hatch and forced her bow three feet out of the water! The seas were slamming into the HETTLER regularly, causing the steamer to "work" on the rocks, and slowly but steadily opening her seams. Blowing his whistle to attract attention, the captain kept his 16-man crew aboard and worked the pumps. The following day, when it was obvious the steamer wasn't going anywhere, they launched their lifeboats, which were towed into Munising by the fishing tug PRE-BLE. From town the captain notified the vessel's owners and wired for assistance from the Great Lakes Towing Company.

After returning to the HETTLER on the 25th, the captain reported her nearly a total loss. She had pounded badly and opened many of her seams. The cargo hold was awash and the salt was rapidly dissolving! The next storm was expected to break the wreck completely. Wrecking tugs were sent for, but they were needed elsewhere to assist newer, more valuable vessels, so the aged steamer was left to fend for herself. This spelled the end for the HERMAN H. HETTLER.

The much-feared storm came on Friday the 26th. The northwester blew for 36 hours and finished off any chance for saving the HETTLER. During the storm, the stern of the steamer broke away and sank and her upper works were completely swept away. When the results of the storm were assessed, she was officially abandoned and turned over to the underwriters. She was a loss of $75,000. Insurance covered all of the cargo loss, but only $40,000 of the vessel's value. The same storm blew the steel freighters THOMAS MAYTHAM and CITY OF BANGOR onto the rocks of Keweenaw Point.

Several years after the wreck, the hull and an old schooner near the Coast Guard station were dynamited by the Coast Guard as hazards to navigation. Today the wreck is scattered over a half mile of lake bottom. On the inner edge of the reef where the HETTLER struck, her boiler can be found in about 25 feet of water, along with part of her hull and a field of debris such as mechanical parts, tanks, piping, and even a bathtub. A few hundred yards to the southwest, two sections of the steamer's sides and the after part of her bottom lie in 10 to 20 feet of water. Deck equipment including her capstan and steam winch lies scattered and broken between the hull pieces. The bow section of her bottom and one of her sides are 200 yards apart several hundred yards south of the rest of the wreckage in 20 to 30 feet of water. The HETTLER's rudder and steering quadrant were salvaged years ago and are on display at the Pictured Rocks National Lakeshore headquarters at Sand Point.

In 1961 a local dive club recovered one of the HETTLER's anchors. After spending more than 30 years as a lawn ornament in Negaunee, Michigan it was returned to the wreck site through the efforts of one of its original salvagers, local divers, and Peter Lindquist of the Alger Underwater Preserve Committee.

The HETTLER had earlier been involved in another Lake Superior shipwreck incident. At 10:30 p.m. on November 5, 1925 she was downbound for Muskegon off Crisp's Point towing the 44-year-old, 187-foot barge JOHN L. CRANE. An 80 mile per hour gale was howling but both vessels seemed to be making fair progress. Without warning the barge suddenly dove for the bottom, tearing out the HETTLER's tow post with a crash. Although the steamer did her best she wasn't able to rescue any of the barge's crew of six men and one woman.

The HERMAN H. HETTLER was built in 1890 in West Bay City by James Davidson and Company for Campbell and Cook of Michigan City, Indiana. In design she was very much a traditional steam barge or, as this style of vessel was called on the lakes, a lumber hooker. Originally named the WALTER VAIL, she was very strongly built, with heavy framing, steel arches in the sides, diagonal steel strapping and an especially robust bow for punching through ice. A 485 horse-power fore-and-aft compound steam engine provided the power. She measured 200 feet in length, 35 feet in beam, 13.3 feet in depth and 726.33 gross tons. The VAIL was valued at $80,000 and had a capacity of a million board feet of lumber.

During her lifetime she had various owners. In the spring of 1913, she was sold to the Herman H. Hettler Lumber Company of Chicago, thus acquiring her final name. Ten years later the steamer was purchased by the Wenonah Transportation Company of Michigan City.

COORDINATES: . . . . .46°28.96' N 86°36.02' W
DEPTH: . . . . .10 - 35 feet

REFERENCES:

Annual Report of the Lake Carrier's Association, 1925, p. 125; 1926, pp. 63-65.

Mining Journal (Marquette, Michigan), October 10, 1961.

Log of the U.S. Coast Guard Station at Grand Marais, November 24, 1926. National Archives. Record Group 26.

Munising News, November 26, December 3, 1926.

U.S. Coast Guard Report of Casualty, Steamer H.H. HETTLER. National Archives. Record Group 26.

Wells, op. cit., p. 75.

KIOWA
November 30, 1929

The steel freighter KIOWA was downbound from Duluth to Chicago with a cargo of flax seed when she was overtaken by a fierce north storm accompanied by a freezing blizzard. Soon the ship was coated with several inches of ice. In the midst of the blow, her cargo shifted, giving the steamer a heavy list and allowing torrents of water to pour in through submerged deck openings. Helpless, the stricken KIOWA drifted before the seas.

Panicked and apparently deciding that all was lost, Captain Alex T. Young ordered ten of the crew into one of the lifeboats while the sinking KIOWA was still drifting helplessly northwest of Au Sable Light. The rest of her crew of 23 were left aboard to shift for themselves. During the launching, one of the supporting lines snapped, upending the boat and spilling the men into the mountainous seas. One man was able to claw his way back into the lifeboat, while six others

The KIOWA.

were pulled back aboard the KIOWA. The rest, including Captain Young, disappeared into the foaming water and the icy grasp of death. Meanwhile the KIOWA continued to drift down the Michigan coast. The mate, Arthur Kronk, left in charge by the "abdication" of the captain, tried to keep order among the near-panicked crew. With death staring them all in the eye, it wasn't easy. Through the long, dark night the dying KIOWA drifted on.

The next day, December 1, at 3:15 p.m., the Coast Guard crew at Grand Marais was busy repairing their submarine telephone cable when they heard the Au Sable Point fog signal blowing several long and short blasts, a prearranged call of distress. Dropping the repair job, the Coast Guard crew manned the power lifeboat and headed for the light station. The blizzard had left deep snow drifts, ruling out any attempt at getting there over land. The lake, although storm-tossed and frigid, was still the best route available. At 4:30 p.m. they arrived at the light and learned from the keeper that the KIOWA had fetched up on the reef to the west of the station.

The KIOWA had originally been spotted by Richard Chilson and his son Charles, who were deer hunting west of Au Sable Point. They were waiting out the storm with their small gas powered motor boat pulled safely up on the beach at the Hurricane River when they sighted the stranded KIOWA. Charles Chilson and his hunting partner Earl Howay bravely launched their boat and made their way out to the steamer. With great difficulty in the rolling seas, they took aboard as many of the crew as they could safely carry, landed them at the lighthouse dock and headed back for more. When the Coast Guard boat finally arrived, Chilson and Howay were bringing in their second load of survivors. The Coast Guard took these men aboard their lifeboat, then proceeded back to the wreck and removed the rest of the KIOWA's crew.

The official Coast Guard log is crystal clear in all aspects of the KIOWA disaster except that concerning exactly how the survivors were actually rescued from the ship. The log gives the impression that the Coast Guard crew, after arriving at the lighthouse and learning of the wreck, then proceeded to the KIOWA and rescued the sixteen crewmen. The official telegram to the Commander of the Eleventh Coast Guard District notifying him of the wreck gave the Coast Guard crew the credit, stating, "picked off 16 men from steamer KIOWA, five lost, one body recovered." Whether the ambiguity was intentional to cover the embarrassment of the Coast Guard in "missing" a major rescue is debatable. Regardless, the Coast Guard crew returned to the Grand Marais Station with the survivors at 7:30 p.m. Since local hotel space could not be found, the bedraggled survivors were quartered at the Coast Guard station.

The KIOWA's drifting lifeboat was discovered about 2 p.m. by the Grand Marais fishing tug JOSEPHINE ADDISON. In it was the frozen body of one of the crew. Although the man had regained the lifeboat after it capsized, he couldn't protect himself from the piercing winds and terrible cold. As a result of hypothermia, he froze to death.

There was no immediate respite for the Coast Guardsmen. At midnight on December 2, the station watchman sighted a steamer off the harbor entrance making distress signals. Immediately the station fired a Coston signal in answer, and launched the power lifeboat. Reaching the steamer, which turned out to be the GEORGE H. DONOVAN, the crew was requested to pilot her into the harbor for shelter. The job was completed with dispatch.

At 6 p.m., Dr. Scholtes, the Alger County coroner, arrived at the station from Munising, quickly impaneled a jury and held an inquest for the recovered body. Subsequently it was identified as that of Max Westerberg, one of the KIOWA's crew. The good doctor also gave the survivors a quick examination and determined that two required further treatment and should return with him to the Munising hospital.

On Tuesday the 3rd, the Coast Guard crew took the power lifeboat with the smaller surfboat in tow and returned to Au Sable Light. Since the lake was still rolling, they anchored the lifeboat about a quarter mile out and used the oar-powered surfboat to run the breakers and make a safe landing on the sandy beach. There they took aboard the marooned hunters and one of the KIOWA's crew who had been left behind in the initial confusion. The trip back through the breakers in the small surfboat was very difficult, since the boat and oars had badly iced up in the freezing weather. They all arrived safe back at the Grand Marais Station but had to break ice all the way from the harbor entrance to the Coast Guard dock.

Heavy weather prevented the KIOWA's underwriters from getting out to their vessel until December 7 when a lull allowed the Coast guard to ferry them out to the wreck. Earlier, on the 5th, an attempt was made using the tug ADDISON but she was driven back by a strong northwest sea. After the vessel and her cargo were examined for over an hour, the underwriters and hull inspectors felt both were a total loss in excess of $200,000.

For several years following the wreck, the whitefish population in the Grand Marais area is said to have increased dramatically, since the fish thrived on the flax seed oils and proteins. Local fishermen shipped large quantities down to Chicago markets, which was just as well since the fish reportedly tasted strongly of linseed oil.

Immediately following the wreck, some salvage was made, especially of her useable tackle, deck machinery and other valuables. During World War II, much of the steel superstructure and part of the hull was salvaged for scrap. However, a great amount of the vessel still remains. Lying in only 30 feet of water on a sand bottom, on a clear day the huge sections of hull are easily visible from the surface. Closest to shore and standing the highest off the bottom is the stern of the wreck, lying over on its port side. Here the diver can see the steamer's steering quadrant and emergency steering gear. A short distance forward, an enclosed ladderway leads down toward the propeller shaft tunnel. At the forward end of the tunnel, the propeller shaft and its massive thrust bearing can be seen. The engine once stood in this area, but salvagers and winter's ice have battered it nearly beyond recognition. The surrounding field of engine room debris includes numerous pumps, generators, valves, and piping of all descriptions. Nearby lie the remains of one of the KIOWA's boilers, with its brass and copper fittings polished by Lake Superior's ever-shifting sands.

Forward of the engine and boiler spaces, the wreckage consists mainly of hull and deck plating, until the diver reaches the bow of the wreck, some distance to the left of the rest of the hulk. The bow lies tipped up on its stem, with its anchor windlass still in place and the anchor chain spilling out of its chain locker. The forward cargo handling mast lies nearby.

Mate Arthur Kronk's involvement in Lake Superior shipwreck didn't end with the wreck of the KIOWA. On May 27, 1933, he was the mate of the 259-foot passenger steamer GEORGE M. COX when she plowed dead into Isle Royale's Rock of Ages Reef in a fog. Mate Kronk was on watch when she hit and was subsequently blamed during the investigation for not keeping the proper course.

Following the example of the KIOWA's captain, Kronk was also the first man off the COX, leaving in a lifeboat with a single female passenger. Seeing his mate about to depart the vessel, the captain

The KIOWA wreck site.   Courtesy of the NPS Submerged
                              Cultural Resources Unit

A diver explores the KIOWA bow winch. FREDERICK STONEHOUSE

ordered him back, instructing him to make certain his boat was properly filled before leaving. When Kronk left again, he had carefully loaded his boat with 17 souls, all women. Evidently he thought he would be stranded on the island for a long, long time!

The KIOWA was the product of an emergency shipbuilding program started during World War I to provide large numbers of deep-sea freighters to help replace submarine losses. Many were built at Great Lakes yards. Under the program a total of 331 similar vessels were eventually constructed. Although the program continued for a time after the war ended, in 1920 it was canceled, leaving many shipyards with unfinished vessels on the ways. With private financing twenty of these vessels were finished in the hope of selling them at a profit. The KIOWA was one of the twenty. Built in 1920 by the Detroit Shipbuilding Company in Wyandotte for the Independent Steamship Company, she measured 251 feet in length, 43 feet in beam, 24 feet in depth and 2,309 gross tons. The KIOWA was built with four watertight bulkheads, a double bottom water ballasting system, two holds forward and two aft. Although starkly different from a traditional lake vessel in

A diver explores the remains of the KIOWA.   FREDERICK STONEHOUSE

appearance, she was able to trade successfully in package freight and some bulk cargo. The KIOWA was powered by a three cylinder, triple expansion steam engine built by the Detroit Shipbuilding Company. Cylinders were 20, 33 and 54 inches in diameter with a 40 inch stroke. Providing 1,250 horsepower, it was sufficient for a steady nine knots. Dual 13-foot by 11-foot Scotch boilers furnished the steam. Her normal complement was seven officers and 15 crewmen.

The KIOWA and one of her twins, the CAYUGA, were sold to the O.W. Blodgett Company of Bay City in the spring of 1927. The following July 23, the KIOWA went hard aground on a Parisienne Island reef, near Whitefish Bay during a fog. Her hull was badly damaged, costing $30,000 to repair.

COORDINATES: . . . . .46°38.72' N 86°13.22' W
DEPTH: . . . . .30 feet

REFERENCES:

Annual Report of the Lake Carriers Association, 1930, p. 54.

Reverend Edward J. Dowling, *Know Your Lakers of World War I* (Sault Ste. Marie, Michigan: Marine Publishing Company, 1978), pp. 43, 91-93.

Grand Marais Pilot & Pictured Rocks Gazette (Grand Marais, Michigan), April 20, May 4, 1983.

Letter, Axel Niemi, to author, March 15, 1977.

Log of Au Sable Light Station. December 1, 1929. National Archives, Record Group 26.

Log of the Grand Marais Coast Guard Station. December 1-7, 1929. National Archives, Record Group 26.

Daily Mining Journal (Marquette, Michigan), July 25, 1928; December 2-6, 1929.

Wells, op. cit., p. 80.

Wreck Report, Steamer KIOWA, December 1, 1929. National Archives, Record Group 26.

Wright, op. cit., p. 204.

NIAGARA
August 29, 1989

Another addition to the Pictured Rocks shipwreck fleet was that of the 200-foot dredge barge NIAGARA. The barge was in tow of the 96-foot tug WILLAM DUGAN and enroute from the Soo to Duluth when heavy weather was encountered west of Grand Island. Both were owned by B & B Contracting of Duluth. Only small craft warnings were in the forecast, but the two vessels encountered 20-foot seas that punished them unmercifully. Unable to even make headway against the winds, the tug and barge were actually pushed backwards. It was all the captain of the DUGAN could do to hold his tow into the piling northwest waves. As it was the combers regularly broke over the pair. The men on the tug feared for their lives, not only from the surging waves but also from the knowledge that if the barge dove for the bottom it would surely drag the tug down with it. Luckily the NIAGARA was unmanned. At dawn on the 29th, when the pair was about 13 miles north of Grand Island, it became apparent the barge was soon going to go down. Reluctantly they slipped the tow line. Within 28 seconds the barge rolled, pitched her stack into the water and plunged for the bottom, 750 feet below.

REFERENCES:

Interview, Mr. Billington, April 22, 1996.

Mining Journal (Marquette, Michigan), August 30, 1989.

STEVEN M. SELVICK
June 1, 1996

Unlike the rest of the shipwrecks along the Pictured Rocks, which were victims of storm, collision, fog, or fire, the latest addition to the area's family of wrecks sank as a result of years of hard work by dedicated volunteers.

When Public Act 184 authorized the establishment of bottomland preserves in Michigan, the main concern was to protect existing shipwrecks. Public Act 452 in 1988 modified the law to allow one vessel "associated with Great Lakes maritime history" to be intentionally sunk in each preserve to serve as a dive attraction.

In 1990 the Keweenaw Bottomland Preserve became the first preserve to take advantage of the new law. The USCGC MESQUITE, a 180-foot Coast Guard buoy tender, had wrecked on a shallow reef off Keweenaw Point on December 4, 1989. The next summer, a commercial salvage firm lifted the MESQUITE off the reef and carried it about a mile to its final resting place off Keystone Bay where it was lowered to the bottom in 110 feet of water.

For years the members of the Alger Underwater Preserve Committee searched for a suitable vessel to sink in the Alger preserve. Finally, in early 1994, Preserve Committee President Peter Lindquist got word that Selvick Marine and Towing of Sturgeon Bay, Wisconsin was planning to scrap their tug STEVEN M. SELVICK. Lindquist contacted the company and suggested that they donate the tug to the preserve, to which Selvick readily agreed.

The tug was built in 1915 in Cleveland, Ohio for the Great Lakes Towing Company. A "city class" tug, she was originally named the LORAIN and was equipped with a 1889-vintage steam engine removed from another vessel. In 1953, the tug was sold to the Merritt - Chapman - Scott Company and renamed the CABOT. Her old steam engine was scrapped, and she was re-powered with a diesel engine. As the CABOT, she served on the construction of the Mackinac Bridge in 1957. The tug was purchased by the Selvick Marine and Towing

Company in 1988. She was re-fitted with a newer Fairbanks-Morse diesel engine and renamed the STEVEN M. SELVICK in honor of the son of the company's owner.

By the time the SELVICK was donated to the Preserve, she had been mothballed for several years and was no longer able to sail under her own power, so it was necessary to tow the tug from Sturgeon Bay to Munising via Lake Michigan, the Straits of Mackinac, northern Lake Huron, the St. Marys River, the Soo Locks and Lake Superior. Mike Kohut of Recreational Diving in Royal Oak, Michigan donated the use of the dive charter boat REC DIVER to make the tow. Despite the fact that they were towing a 71-foot, 74-ton tugboat with a 42-foot passenger boat, Lindquist and his volunteer crew managed to bring the SELVICK to port in Munising without mishap.

Once at the dock in her final port, the real work on the tug began. In order to avoid polluting the lake, hundreds of gallons of fuel oil and lubricants had to be pumped out of the tug's tanks and bilges, and the interior was steam-cleaned. Miscellaneous equipment such as auxiliary engines and generators had to be removed to give divers safe access to the engine room. Volunteers from the local area and around the Midwest accomplished these jobs over the course of two years. Approval from the Coast Guard and the Army Corps of Engineers was needed to ensure that the sunken tug would not pose a hazard to navigation.

Late in the winter of 1995, a through-hull fitting deep inside the SELVICK froze and ruptured, allowing water to pour into the bilges. As the deep-hulled tug settled to the bottom, she rolled over nearly 45 degrees onto her starboard side before coming to rest with her gunwale and cabin hatches below water. When Lindquist and friends tried to pump out the water, the tug merely rolled farther over on her side. Drastic action was needed! Calls went out to divers across the Upper Peninsula and Wisconsin, and on a sunny Saturday in April a volunteer crew went to work to raise the tug. While one crew cleared sand from under the boat's keel, another group fastened heavy-duty lift bags to the sunken side of the boat. Another group of divers buried heavy anchors off to the side of the tug and ran stout lines to the top of the pilothouse to help pull her upright. With several pumps draining water from inside the hull, divers stuffed plastic into every leak in the superstructure. Finally, with the addition of more pumps, the SELVICK slowly righted herself and floated free of the bottom.

On the morning of June 1, 1996 the SELVICK was slowly towed out the east channel by the U.S. Forest Service tug ABRAHAM WILLIAMS, accompanied by a flotilla of small boats as well as chartered vessels with VIPs, media representatives and spectators on board. Once at the sinking site, some six miles north of Munising off Grand Island's Trout Point, her flag was lowered for the last time and workers opened valves below the waterline to flood the vessel. When this flow proved too small to sink the vessel in a reasonable time, pumps aboard one of the support vessels were used to pump water into the tug's hull. Finally, with her deck awash, lake water began to pour aboard through her hatches, and it was only a matter of seconds before the STEVEN M. SELVICK sank stern first, disappearing to lie beneath the waves in her final resting place.

The STEVEN M. SELVICK as she slowly fills

FREDERICK STONEHOUSE

She's gone... FREDERICK STONEHOUSE

The SELVICK came to rest on a sandstone bottom 60 feet deep, and sits upright with a list to port. Damage to the tug from the sinking was minimal: the rudder broke off when it hit the bottom, and all the glass was blown out of the pilothouse windows. Divers have access to all areas of the tug; doors were secured in the open position and a hatch was cut in her deck to provide access to the machinery spaces in the stern. The pilothouse, galley, messroom, engineroom, and crew quarters can all be penetrated.

COORDINATES: . . . . .46°29.53' N 86°35.87' W
DEPTH: . . . . .60 feet

REFERENCES:

Rod DesJardins, *"The Final Voyage of the STEVEN M. SELVICK,"* Action Shopper, (Marquette, Michigan) May 2, 1996, p. 1.

Mining Journal (Marquette, Michigan), June 2, 1996.

Frederick Stonehouse, *Shipwreck of the MESQUITE,* (Duluth, Minnesota: Lake Superior Port Cities, 1991)

CHAPTER THREE

RESCUES AND RECOVERIES

LADY ELGIN
August, 1858

Early in August, 1858 the elegant sidewheel steamer LADY ELGIN stranded on Au Sable Reef, where she lay for two days before being pulled off by the steamer ILLINOIS. She received an estimated $1,400 in damages. The LADY ELGIN had stranded earlier in the season off Copper Harbor during a gale and sustained $8000 in damages, a considerable amount for 1858.

The LADY ELGIN achieved infamy in the early morning hours of September 8, 1860 when she sank on Lake Michigan. The steamer collided with the schooner AUGUSTA ten miles off Winnetka, Illinois, about sixteen miles north of Chicago while carrying about 350 passengers and a crew of 35. The LADY ELGIN sank within 20 minutes, taking an estimated 300 souls with her.

REFERENCES:

Detroit Daily Free Press, August 12, 14, 1858

Lytle and Holdcamper, *Merchant Vessels,* p. 123.

Mansfield, op. cit., pp. 683-687.

Wells, op. cit., p.3.

WILLIAMS SAILBOAT
June 2, 1859

An especially tragic disaster occurred on June 2, 1859. On that date three young people from Grand Island, Christopher C. Williams, his sister Saphronia and their cousin William Clark, sailed to Marquette for a day of shopping. On the return trip they ran into a strong south gale accompanied by rain and sleet, and were forced far out into the lake. They were last sighted fighting their way along in high seas by the keeper of the North Light.

Later, when the wind shifted to the north and the storm abated, the boat was discovered ashore split in two. The bodies were never recovered. Locally the accident became known as the "North Light Disaster."

REFERENCES:

Beatrice Hanscom Castle, *The Grand Island Story* (Marquette, Michigan: The John M. Longyear Research Library, 1974), pp. 61-63.

Lake Superior Journal (Marquette, Michigan), June 8, 15, 1859.

EVELINE BATES
November 10, 1869

The two-masted schooner EVELINE BATES was moored to the Bay Furnace dock near the west entrance to Grand Island Harbor when a strong north squall blew her free and onto the beach south of the dock. The BATES had just arrived with a cargo of supplies for the Bay Furnace, most of which were still aboard her at the time of the accident. Since the schooner was in a sheltered spot, it was thought the BATES could be easily pulled off. In spite of the efforts of the Marquette based tug JAY C. MORSE, the BATES wasn't freed until the spring of 1870. She sustained damages of $1,800.

The BATES was built at Huron, Ohio in 1858. She was 233 tons, 128 feet by 26 feet by 10 feet. Owned by E.H. Dykes, her home port was Grand Haven, Michigan. She continued in service until 1896.

REFERENCES:

Mining Journal (Marquette, Michigan), November 13, 25, 1869.
Marine Directory of the Great Lakes. R. Polk & Company, 1897.
Merchant Vessels of the United States, 1897.
Wells, op. cit., p. 7.

DREADNAUGHT
October 28, 1870

The schooner wreck in Murray Bay has long been called the DREADNAUGHT, although in fact it is most likely the BERMUDA. Part of the confusion is undoubtedly caused by historical coincidence since the DREADNAUGHT did at one time wreck in the same general area.

On the morning of Friday, October 28, 1870, the DREAD-NAUGHT, downbound from Marquette with a cargo of ore, went ashore near the southwest corner of Grand Island, across the channel from the Bay Furnace at Onota. Reportedly the schooner was in only seven feet of water and could be pulled off without trouble. The accident was reported by her captain when he returned to Marquette two days later to fetch the tug DUDLEY and a large steam pump. The tug JAY C. MORSE was also engaged to tow the schooner to the Soo once free. Salvage attempts that fall were unsuccessful, and she was abandoned as a total loss. The DREADNAUGHT was left on the reef for the winter, although it is likely that all rigging, chains, anchors and associated gear were recovered.

According to local reports, the wreck could well have been caused by the captain's drunkenness. For two or three days prior to sailing from Marquette, he was said to be in a state of "beastly intoxication" and made a great nuisance of himself. The Mining Journal stated the only reason he wasn't thrown behind bars was the fact that he was the captain and that his presence would have disgraced the county jail! Ominously, he was reputedly still drunk when the DREADNAUGHT finally left port. When he returned for the tugs he was said to be only "partly sober," and after reporting the news of the wreck, he proceeded to celebrate his narrow escape from death in bacchic style. Only with great difficulty was he put aboard the DUDLEY for the return trip to the wreck!

The DREADNAUGHT was successfully recovered the following year but damages totalled an estimated $13,000. The actual salvage was done by the tug GENERAL GRANT. Large steam pumps were used to dewater the DREADNAUGHT enough for the tug to haul her free. Together with the schooner HELFENSTEIN, recently raised from the bottom of Marquette harbor, she was towed to Cleveland for repairs. Built in Oswego, New York in 1856, the schooner was 136 feet in length, 26 feet in beam and 11.4 feet in depth. Her end came on November 28, 1893 off Racine, Wisconsin when she iced over in a gale and foundered. No lives were lost.

REFERENCES:

Detroit Marine Historian, December 1984.

Mining Journal (Marquette, Michigan), September 24, October 1, 8, November 5, 12, 19, 26, 1870.

Stonehouse Files.

Wells, op. cit., p. 8.

PHIL SHERIDAN
October 27, 1875

On October 27, 1875, the 711-ton propeller PHIL SHERIDAN went ashore at Sand Point while trying to enter Grand Island Harbor in a snow storm. At first it was thought that the steamer would prove a total loss, but after her cargo was lightered, the steamer IRA CHAFFEE was able to release her undamaged and she proceeded on her way. A month later, her luck took a turn for the worse. On November 30, en route to Detroit with a cargo of salt, the SHERIDAN caught fire on Lake Erie about 20 miles west of Buffalo. Captain Mitchell and his 23-man crew escaped to the boats, and the steamer burned to the waterline. The men in the boats were rescued by the barge TURNER.

REFERENCES:

Alpena Argus (Alpena, Michigan), December 8, 1875.

Detroit Evening News, October 30, November 5, December 1, 1875.

Milwaukee Daily Sentinel, October 29, November 3, 6, 1875.

Mining Journal (Marquette, Michigan), October 30, November 6, December 11, 1875.

J.K. WHITE
September 28, 1877

In addition to her usual duty of towing rafts of logs on the lake, the 75-foot iron sidewheel steamer J.K. WHITE was used as a salvage tug by David Sang, a hard hat diver from Marquette. In this capacity, she participated in the salvage of many local shipwrecks, including the F. MORRELL at Grand Island and the UNION at Au Sable Point. On September 28, 1876, she became a shipwreck herself, going ashore on Grand Island. She lay there until November 11, 1878 when Sang recovered her and returned her to Marquette. Although nearly everything portable had been stolen from the wreck, her machinery was said to be in good shape and Sang intended to return her to service. However, she remained beached at Marquette for at least three years before passing from the records.

REFERENCES:

Mining Journal (Marquette, Michigan), November 16, 1878; August 14, 1880, December 17, 1881.

MARY MERRITT
September 7, 1881

The MARY MERRITT, a 347-ton, three-masted Canadian schooner under the command of Captain Neil Murray, was caught in a gale and blown on the beach about three miles west of Au Sable Point. The schooner had been loading a cargo of square timber at Sullivan's Landing. All of the crew was saved. The schooner, however, was badly damaged and immediate steps to haul her off with the tug JIM HAYS failed.

Surprisingly, two weeks later the tug WINSLOW pulled her off with little difficulty, and towed her to Detroit for a refit. The MER-RITT was later sold and renamed the DOT. As the DOT, in August of 1883 she sprang a leak and sank off Grand Marais.

REFERENCES:

Detroit Evening News, September 22, 24, 1881.

Mining Journal (Marquette, Michigan), September 10, 1881; September 1, 1883.

MYSTIC
August 4, 1884

Captain Martin Daniels was a well-known figure on the Marquette waterfront. After 13 years (and eight shipwrecks!) on salt water, he started in the shipping business there in 1871. He bought the little 50-foot schooner TOM BOY and started hauling cargos nobody else would touch - such as high explosives from the Marquette powder mills. On August 1, 1880, Captain Daniels and his 15 year old crewman survived the sinking of the TOM BOY near Marquette. Within the month, Daniels had a new vessel, the 65-foot MYSTIC. He continued hauling his hazardous cargos, and occasionally branched out into salvage work

In August, 1884, Daniels was working to recover an anchor and chain lost by the schooner MARY MERRITT when she went ashore near Au Sable Point three years earlier. After they had successfully raised the anchor, a heavy northwester came up. Daniels took his schooner a safe distance offshore and anchored to ride out the storm. At about 4 a.m., the MYSTIC's anchor chain parted, and, before they could make sail, the schooner was blown high and dry on the beach.

Fortunately, the MYSTIC went ashore on a sand beach, and sustained only minimal damage. The tug DUDLEY pulled the schooner off the beach on the 7th, and by the 11th Captain Daniels was again loading a cargo of blasting powder and sailing for the mines of the Copper Country.

After his retirement from the lakes in the late 1890's, Daniels took to prospecting in the hills along the lakeshore north of Marquette. In 1898, he discovered gold and silver and opened a small mine. The following year he found another vein two miles to the north, and opened The Original Sauk's Head Mine. Work at the mine continued until 1904, but Captain Daniels never did strike it rich.

REFERENCES:

Daily Mining Journal (Marquette, Michigan), August 6, 9, 1884.

Daniel R. Fountain, *Michigan Gold: Mining in the Upper Peninsula* (Duluth: Lake Superior Port Cities, Inc., 1992), pp. 105-109.

Mining Journal (Marquette, Michigan), August 16, 1884.

Frederick Stonehouse, *Marquette Shipwrecks* (AuTrain, Michigan: Avery Color Studios, 1977), pp. 18-19.

SOPHIA MINCH
September 30, 1886

The three-masted schooner SOPHIA MINCH, with Captain H.J. Trinter, left Ashland, Wisconsin Monday morning, September 27, in the tow of the steam barge A. EVERETT. That afternoon the steamer broke down while just behind the Apostle Islands. At 10 p.m. the disabled EVERETT found a tow to nearby Washburn, Wisconsin, and left the MINCH with instructions to proceed alone.

The schooner started off with a good wind but just past the Keweenaw she was struck by a southwest gale accompanied by snow squalls. Between Manitou Island and Stannard Rock she was forced to heave to. Later she attempted to run to Marquette for shelter but in the blinding snow was unable to find it!

The MINCH bounded around in the wild lake without a clear idea of her position until Thursday when, without warning, the cliffs of Grand Island loomed before her. She attempted to change her course, but the old schooner began to pound too hard, so she altered her heading to try to sneak in behind the island. But disaster struck and the schooner stranded on the sand spit at the southwest corner of the island.

The schooner, however, was resting easily and sheltered from the seas. The captain made his way to Marquette where he arranged for the tug A.C. ADAMS and a lighter to come to her aid. After removing only a small amount of coal, the tug was able to pull the MINCH free three days later. By this time the EVERETT had arrived on the scene, so she took the MINCH back in tow and they continued on their trip down the lakes.

In this photo, the SOPHIA MINCH is ashore at Ashtabula, Ohio. She also went ashore on the southwest corner of Grand Island.

KEN E. THRO

REFERENCES:

Detroit Evening News, October 2, 5, 1886.

Mining Journal (Marquette, Michigan), October 2, 1886.

REPUBLIC
November 26, 1886

While steam freighters might tow two or three schooner-barges on their trips up and down the lakes, powerful tugs would tow as many as six consorts in a string. One such towing tug was the NIAGARA.

On the morning of November 26, 1886, the NIAGARA steamed out of Marquette harbor towing a single ore-laden schooner-barge. Her other five consorts had finished loading earlier and sailed out of port on a favorable wind, expecting to be picked up and taken in tow later on by the faster tug. Out on the lake that evening, however, a heavy north gale blew up and three of the schooners sought shelter in Grand Island Harbor. Two of them reached safety but the largest, the 139-foot, 314-ton REPUBLIC, ran up on the rocks at Wood Island, just three miles short of refuge. The crew was able to reach shore safely in the yawl.

When the NIAGARA was finally able to reach the REPUBLIC on the 31st, the schooner was found to be wedged among boulders in 10 feet of water with her timbers badly sprung and most of her upper works gone. The Marquette Mining Journal noted that "she is in a very exposed place, and will no doubt prove a total loss." The owners were of a like opinion, and surrendered her to the underwriters.

Surprisingly, the spring of 1887 found the REPUBLIC none the worse for her winter on the rocks. The insurance company contracted with salvagers Parker and Mellen of Detroit to raise the schooner on a "no cure, no pay" basis. The wrecking schooner YOUNG AMERICA proceeded to the wreck and, after lightering only 150 tons of the 496-

ton cargo, pumped her dry and refloated her with a single steam pump. The REPUBLIC was towed to Cleveland and repaired, and was quickly returned to service.

REFERENCES:

Daily Mining Journal (Marquette, Michigan), November 30, December 1, 2, 4, 6, 1886; May 29, 30, June 13, July 1, 2, 18, 25, 1887.

Detroit Evening News, November 29, December 1, 1886; June 29, 1887.

Mining Journal (Marquette, Michigan), April 2, 1887.

RICHARD MORWOOD
November 19, 1887

The RICHARD MORWOOD was en route to Port Arthur, Ontario, with a cargo of 2,500 barrels of oil when a northwest gale blew her off her north shore track and into the high cliffs at the northwest corner of Grand Island. The schooner struck at 11:30 p.m. in the midst of a blinding snow squall. She was driven hard up against the cliffs as if to a dock, and the men were able to simply clamber ashore. Unable to scale the sheer cliffs during the fury of the storm however, they returned to the schooner, where they took shelter from the storm. The vessel held together until the seas subsided on the 21st and allowed the crew of seven to again reach safety on shore.

A Canadian vessel, registered from St. Catharines, Ontario, the schooner was owned by her master, Captain McPherson. The 268-ton MORWOOD was built at Port Dover, Ontario by Waterbury in 1856 and rebuilt in 1874. The schooner, an $8,000 value, was only half insured, although the cargo, owned by Standard Oil, was fully insured.

Soon after the wreck, the Marquette tugs F.W. GILLETT and A.C. ADAMS, together with a scow, began to salvage the cargo. By June of 1888, nearly all of it had been recovered. Since the oil was "Canada

Test," it could not be used in the United States so it was shipped to Winnipeg via rail.

Although the MORWOOD was initially considered to be a total loss, reported to be in a "bad place" with "her bottom full of holes," Marquette salvors recovered her with relative ease in June of 1888. She spent a year beached in shallow water in Marquette harbor before being repaired enough for a trip to a shipyard. Taken to Port Huron in July of 1889, she was rebuilt at a cost of $15,000 and renamed the E.B. PALMER. On November 13, 1892 she foundered off Middle Island, Lake Huron without loss of life.

REFERENCES:

Daily Mining Journal (Marquette, Michigan), November 23, 25, 28, December 1, 1887; June 15, 22, 30, November 16, 1888; July 12, 15, 17, 22, 31, October 3, 12, 1889.

Detroit Evening News, November 22, December 1, 1987; July 2, 1888.

KEEWATIN
October 20, 1888

The KEEWATIN, a Canadian schooner under the command of Captain John Keith, was downbound from the north shore with a cargo of block sandstone when she was mauled by a strong northerly gale. As the gale shifted from northeast to northwest, and back again to northeast, the heavily laden schooner was forced to alter her course each time. In the vicinity of Stannard Rock, the seas tore loose the schooner's yawl, thus stripping her of her only lifeboat.

On Saturday morning, October 20, while trying to enter Grand Island Harbor to shelter from the storm, the KEEWATIN struck a sand bar near William's Landing on Grand Island. Since they had lost their yawl, the captain and crew were forced to remain aboard until Monday, when they were rescued by local men. Taken by train to Marquette, Captain Keith reported the accident.

Fired by the urgency of salvage, the Marquette based tug F.W. GILLETT departed at 4 o'clock the following morning. By 8 a.m. she had completed the trip and was alongside the stranded schooner. Immediately she began to pump her out and to dredge out the sand around her hull. By 9 a.m. Wednesday the KEEWATIN was free. Quick work had cheated the lake of another victim.

REFERENCES:

Daily Mining Journal (Marquette, Michigan), October 23, 1888.

Detroit Evening News, October 23, 24, 1888.

Mining Journal (Marquette, Michigan). October 27, 1888.

EMPIRE STATE
July 17, 1891

The reader can imagine the Au Sable Point lightkeeper's surprise when, at 3:30 a.m. on July 17, 1891 he answered the loud pounding at his front door to find a noisy crowd of 64 passengers and crew from the propeller EMPIRE STATE. The ship had run onto a reef about a mile northwest of the station in the thick fog and the survivors were seeking shelter. All were drenched after wading ashore from the lifeboats.

The 24 passengers stayed at the light until 8:00 p.m. the next night when the propeller INDIA picked them up. The steamer's 40 man crew remained two days longer. Doubtless throughout the period, the lightkeeper's routine was severely impacted, as was his food supply!

The EMPIRE STATE had actually hit the reef at about 7:00 p.m. After hearing an unusual echo from his whistle, Captain Green ordered her course changed two points to the north to stand well clear of Au

The steamer EMPIRE STATE. The wooden arches were used to provide additional stiffening to the hull.   KEN E. THRO

Sable, but it was too late. She struck almost immediately after his command. Since the weather was calm, the captain tried to get off himself but his pumps were not equal to the task. When the wind came up later, he abandoned his ship and safely put all passengers and crew ashore.

At first it was believed the propeller was a goner - but fortune smiled on the old girl. The wrecking tug FAVORITE with wrecking master Captain Martin Swain and Detroit diver John Quinn were able to respond quickly. Quinn put temporary patches on the holes, lightered nearly half of her cargo, then used two big steam pumps to dewater her. Being heavy with freight, including over 700 tons of copper, the EMPIRE STATE had settled fast to the bottom. But Quinn did his work well. On July 22, she was afloat and on her way to the Soo for temporary repairs. She then proceeded under her own power to Buffalo. Two years previous, Quinn had also worked on the SMITH MOORE salvage evaluation.

The EMPIRE STATE's career was inordinately long, lasting until 1916, a period of 55 years. It was an incredible life-span for a wooden hull. The 210-foot, 860-ton propeller was built by Charles S. Bidwell in Buffalo in 1862. When she slid down the ways on April 5, it was a major event with a very large crowd attending. Following the ceremony, a king-sized lunch was served in celebration.

The EMPIRE STATE was a crack passenger propeller for many years, a reliable link to the lake ports for both passengers and freight. A traveller on her to Lake Superior in 1880 noted, "...the appointments of the steamers of this line are the finest I have seen on any steamers in America, having all the accommodations of first class hotels, bathrooms, barber shops, etc. While the officers and waiters are simply perfection in their courtesy, there is not many passengers on board thereby adding to the comfort. Quite a number of immigrants on board on the lower deck. Took massive machinery for Superior Mining district."

REFERENCES:

Annual Report of the United States Life-Saving Service, 1892 (Washington, D.C.: Government Printing Office), p. 184.

John C. Carter, "A Journey on the Great Lakes 1880," *Telescope,* January-February 1981, p. 15.

Daily Mining Journal (Marquette, Michigan), July 20, 22, 24, 25, 1891.

Detroit Free Press, July 18, 19, 20, 23, 1891.

Erik Heyl, *Early American Steamers,* Volume III (Buffalo: Erik Heyl, 1964), pp. 129-130.

Log of the Au Sable Light Station, July 17-23, 1891. National Archives, Record Group 26.

NELSON
September 29, 1895

On the same day the ELMA met her end on the Pictured Rocks, a minor casualty occurred to the schooner-barge NELSON. The NELSON, together with the schooner-barge MARY B. MITCHELL, was in tow of the steamer A. FOLSOM when they experienced trouble in entering Munising's west channel. The FOLSOM and her charges were upbound light from Cleveland to Marquette. They were struggling to round the southwest point of Grand Island when the high seas caused the schooners to drift towards the beach. To prevent them from going aground, Captain Millard of the FOLSOM signaled for the schooners to drop their anchors until the wind abated. The NELSON's crew was too slow, however, and she stranded in the shallow water on the west side of Powell Point, near the range lights. Although the NELSON was firmly aground in only five feet of water, water deep enough to float her was a bare fifty feet away.

The big schooner NELSON, before being cut down to a schooner-barge.
KEN E. THRO

The NELSON wasn't in an exposed position and should have been easily released, but she wasn't recovered until more than two weeks later. The tug CHAMPION worked on the schooner all day on the 12th and managed to drag her 10 feet toward deeper water, but broke all her tow lines in the process. The tug SWAIN was dispatched from Marquette with a new hawser. Again the CHAMPION went to work, but this time she broke her propeller and had to limp to port for repairs. The SWAIN took over the recovery effort and on October 15 pulled the schooner free, but not before she had broken her own tow post. The FOLSOM took the recalcitrant NELSON in tow and brought her to Marquette. After minor repairs to a damaged rudder, she loaded a cargo of ore and continued her career.

The NELSON was later lost in a tragic Lake Superior shipwreck on May 13, 1899. She was again with the MITCHELL in tow of the FOLSOM when they were struck by a freezing northwest gale off Grand Marais. In the heavy weather the NELSON's tow line parted. Although the schooner was able to set enough sail to keep her head to the wind, she was badly beaten by the waves and her decks and rigging were covered with ice. When it became certain that his vessel was lost, the captain placed his five-man crew and his wife and daughter into the yawl. He then stayed aboard to swing out the davits.

When the boat was safely launched and secured to the schooner by the bow line, the captain jumped for the wildly bobbing yawl but missed and landed in the lake. Surfacing, he saw the schooner raise her stern high into the air and then plunge quickly for the bottom, dragging the yawl and its occupants down with it by the still-attached line. Before his horrified eyes his wife and daughter, as well as his five-man crew, drowned! The captain survived and later floated ashore near Deer Park.

The NELSON was built in 1866. At the time of her loss she was valued at approximately $10,000.

REFERENCES:

Annual Report of the United States Life-Saving Service, 1900 (Washington, D.C.: Government Printing Office), p. 179.

Beeson's, op. cit., p. 139.

Cleveland Plain Dealer, October 2, 1895.

Daily Mining Journal (Marquette, Michigan), October 1, 4, 9, 18, 21, 23, 1895.

Detroit Evening News, October 1, 2, 13, 14, 16, 1895.

Journal of the Lighthouse at Whitefish Point, May 1899. National Archives. Record Group 26.

Journal of the Crisp Point Life-Saving Station, May 14-19, 1899. National Archives. Record Group 26.

Journal of the Muskallonge Lake Life-Saving Station, May 14-20, 1899. National Archives. Record Group 26.

Journal of the Vermilion Point Life-Saving Station, May 14, 1899. National Archives. Record Group 26.

ESCANABA
November 25, 1898

November voyages on Lake Superior have always been fraught with dangers, but the threat of the cargo exploding was not among the sailors' usual concerns. It was quite the contrary for the crew of the steam freighter ESCANABA, however. On the afternoon of November 25, 1898, the ESCANABA was running into the east channel to Grand Island Harbor when a heavy snow storm obscured all landmarks. The skipper tried to maintain his course by dead reckoning, but at about 4:30 the steamer ran hard aground on the rocky reef jutting into the channel two miles northeast of the East Channel Light. In addition to her cargo of salt and general merchandise, the ESCANABA carried a number of carboys of nitroglycerin.

Although the glass jugs were padded with straw and enclosed in wooden crates, too strong a jolt could detonate the unstable explosive. Fortunately, no explosion followed the impact on the reef.

A quick inspection showed little damage, but the steamer was sitting five feet out of the water at the bow. Although the crew jettisoned 2000 barrels of salt from her cargo, she remained stuck fast on the reef. Tugs were sent to assist the ESCANABA and they carefully lightered her delicate cargo of nitroglycerin and the rest of the general merchandise. Still the tugs were unable to budge her. Finally, late on the 26th, she was pulled free by the passing steamer NORTH STAR. Essentially undamaged by her ordeal, the ESCANABA proceeded to take on a load of lumber and returned down the lakes.

REFERENCES:

Alger County Republican (Munising, Michigan), November 26, December 3, 1898.

Daily Mining Journal (Marquette, Michigan), November 28, 1898.

Detroit Evening News, November 27, 1898.

COMMODORE
November 14, 1900

The storm gods of the lake are not only powerful, but also fickle, sometimes claiming vessels that seemed impervious to disaster and on other occasions sparing those that are ripe for the taking. One example of the lake's mercurial behavior is illustrated by the trials of the schooner-barge COMMODORE.

The COMMODORE, in the tow of the steamer ELIZA H. STRONG, was bound for Portage Lake when the pair ran into a fierce storm after passing Whitefish Point. Both vessels carried cargos of coal

The schooner-barge COMMODORE. Note the large deck load, cut-down masts and donkey engine forward.   Ken E. Thro

consigned to the Centennial Mining Company. During the storm, the tow line parted and the COMMODORE was blown away from the steamer.

Battered by the waves and torn apart by the winds, the schooner was reduced to little more than a floating wreck. Her sails were gone, her rudder carried away, and the deck cargo had been swept off into the rolling seas. The crew decided their vessel was doomed! Launching their small yawl boat, the crew hurriedly abandoned the COMMODORE. Their exit was so fast, the captain left many valuables in his cabin. There was no doubt in the crew's mind that they would never see their trusty vessel afloat again. If she didn't sink outright, she would surely be blown ashore or into the deadly cliffs of the Pictured Rocks. The crew was later picked up by the STRONG, which was searching for the missing COMMODORE.

To the crew's complete surprise, the next day the steamer located the COMMODORE still afloat, although badly disabled. Since the storm had moderated considerably, the STRONG was able to take the COMMODORE in tow and bring her safely into Munising. The COMMODORE was left there for quick repairs while the STRONG continued on to Portage Lake.

REFERENCE:

Daily Mining Journal (Marquette). November 16, 20, 1900.

CHARLES H. BRADLEY, BRIGHTIE, MARY WOOLSON
November 18, 1900

Some shipwrecks occurred not in fact, but only in people's imaginations. A case in point is the "foundering" of two schooners on November 18, 1900.

At 11 a.m. on November 18, Captain Henry Cleary, the keeper of the Marquette Life-Saving Station, received a telephone message from Munising to the effect that two schooners were sunk in the channel between Grand Island and the mainland and that the crews were desperately clinging to the rigging.

Cleary immediately organized his crew and secured a special South Shore train for the run to Munising. Rapidly the well-drilled life-saving crew loaded the surfboat, car and beach apparatus onto two flat cars. Since a coach was not available, the life-saving crew simply took their normal seats in the surfboat and rode it as if they were riding the waves!

As luck would have it, their trip was not to be. Just as the train was leaving the rail yard, a message came through that the tug J.W. WARD had rescued the men from the schooners. After unloading their gear, the life-saving crew returned to their station. It was the first time in the 1900 fall season they had been called out.

Two days later the mystery of the two strange schooners was cleared up. It seems that Captain Pecord of the tug WARD had discovered the steamer CHARLES H. BRADLEY, with the schooner-barges BRIGHTIE and MARY WOOLSON in trouble off Grand Island. Apparently a small storm was blowing and the steamer was having engine trouble and thus impaired, was unable to bring herself or the tow to safety. The tug towed all three into a safe anchorage at Munising harbor.

There never was a wreck, nor were the life-savers needed. The vessels were not in peril, other than perhaps of blowing ashore.

The tug WARD, together with the tug PETREL, had earlier departed Marquette for Munising with a large raft of cedar logs. Only luck placed her in Munising and allowed her to earn a fat $300 towing fee for her owners.

The schooner-barge BRIGHTIE.   KEN E. THRO

The vessels were owned by O.W. Blodgett of West Bay City. Although they survived their close call at Grand Island, all three of them eventually succumbed to shipwreck. The MARY WOOLSON, built in 1888, sank in 1920 on Lake Huron after colliding with the BRADLEY, which once again had her in tow. The BRIGHTIE met her end on Lake Michigan in 1928 after 60 years of service when her tired seams gave way, overwhelming her pumps. The 804-ton BRADLEY, built in 1890, ended her days in 1931 at Portage Lake when she was destroyed by fire.

REFERENCES:

Daily Mining Journal (Marquette, Michigan), November 17, 19, 20, 1900.

Detroit Evening News, November 19, 1900.

ELIZA H. STRONG
August 31, 1901

The same 205-foot, 781-ton steamer ELIZA H. STRONG that was involved in the COMMODORE incident in 1900 later became a storm casualty in the same area. The steamer was again towing the COMMODORE when they were struck by a storm 20 miles east of Stannard Rock on Thursday, August 29, 1901. This time it was the STRONG that took the worse pounding. As she was battered by the seas, the steamer sprang an uncontrollable leak. Within half an hour she became waterlogged and seemed ready to go down at any minute. The twelve crewmen abandoned ship and boarded the COMMODORE, which ran before the wind for shelter at Munising, arriving there Friday evening. That same night, the steamer MUELLER nearly collided with the derelict steamer in the fog. Although still afloat, the STRONG was a pitiful sight, with her after cabin gone and her deck load of lumber washed away. With the storm abated and the seas subsiding, the MUELLER took the abandoned steamer in tow and brought her into Munising harbor, much to the amazement of her crew on board the COMMODORE. They were certain she had sank! The STRONG was run aground and allowed to settle in shallow water.

A few weeks later wrecker Harris Baker with the tug CHAMPION pumped her out and discovered that a burst pipe had caused her original flooding. After repairs she was returned to service. The steamer with her cargo of lumber was appraised at $10,000, giving a salvage award of about $3000 to the MUELLER. The STRONG was built in 1899 and owned by the Strong Transportation Company of Tonawanda, New York. She ended her career on October 25, 1904 when she caught fire and foundered in Lake Huron off Lexington, Michigan.

REFERENCES:

Daily Mining Gazette (Houghton, Michigan), September 21, 1901.

Daily Mining Journal (Marquette, Michigan), September 2, 7, 25, October 8, 1901.

Detroit Evening News, August 31, September 4, 28, October 8, December 14, 1901.

Duluth News-Tribune, December 15, 1901.

Mining Journal (Marquette, Michigan), October 5, 1901.

CRESCENT CITY AND BARGE NO. 130
April 9, 1902

Both the 406-foot steel steamer CRESCENT CITY and the 292-foot whaleback barge No. 130 were aground on Au Sable Reef from April 9th through the 12th. They were downbound from Marquette with the year's first cargos of iron ore when a fog bank rolled in from the southwest, obscuring dreaded Au Sable Point.

Although the lighthouse keeper started firing up the steam-powered fog whistle at 6 a.m., not enough pressure had been built up to start it blowing before both vessels struck the reef at 6:15 a.m.

To assist the stranded vessels the lighthouse keeper delivered a message to nearby Grand Marais calling for tugs and men to jettison the ore cargo.

The Grand Marais life-savers soon arrived at the wreck site just in case their assistance was needed. Their lookout had sighted the stranded vessels at 7:40 a.m. when the fog lifted enough to allow him to see the nine and a half miles distance to the reef. Always willing to pitch in to save a vessel in distress, the life-savers went to work shovelling overboard part of the iron ore cargo. Later they were joined by hired men from Grand Marais. In all, nearly 100 men worked for two days to jettison the ore, one shovelful at a time.

On April 10th, the tug GENERAL arrived on the scene but could not dislodge either the CRESCENT CITY or the barge. Two days later another tug joined in and together they hauled the steamer free at 3 p.m. Finally at 9 a.m. the next day the barge was also freed.

Since the barge was leaking badly and a gale had started to howl, the CRESCENT CITY towed her to shelter at Grand Island for hasty repairs rather than try to continue the planned trip down the lakes. Because of the imminent possibility of the barge foundering, the life-savers accompanied them in their small surfboat towed astern of the barge. The forty mile trip lasted seven hours and was certainly a wet and cold one for the life-savers. Stranded by the gale at Grand Island, they didn't get back to their station until midnight on the 14th. Luckily they were able to hitch a tow back from the tug GENERAL, saving themselves a very long, hard row.

When examined by a diver, the barge was found to have stove in one of her forward plates and only the still-intact collision bulkhead had kept her from flooding. Once the hole was patched, the barge's own pumps were sufficient to keep the water down.

The CRESCENT CITY was built at South Chicago, Illinois in 1897. She later became a major wreck on Lake Superior on November

28, 1905 when she crashed against the cliffs north of Duluth during a terrible gale. She was eventually recovered at a cost of $100,000.

Barge No. 130 was built at West Superior in 1893. Renamed the LYNN in 1911, she was scrapped in 1924.

REFERENCES:

Annual Report of the United States Life-Saving Service, 1903 (Washington, D.C.: Government Printing Office), p. 145.

Daily Mining Journal (Marquette, Michigan), April 12, 14, 1902.

Detroit Evening News, April 8, 12, 13, 20, 1902.

Log of Au Sable Light Station, April 9-12, 1902. National Archives, Record Group 26.

John K. Wilterding, *McDougall's Dream,* the American Whaleback (Duluth: Lakeside Publications, 1969), pp. 46-47.

LIZZIE A. LAW
May 9, 1902

A basic problem faced by the old schooners was the very elemental one of leaking. Some of the elderly vessels often developed an unholy appetite for water. It was not uncommon to have a large amount of it sloshing about in the hold, especially during heavy weather when seams were working. All of the water, of course, had to be pumped out by the crews. In earlier days, when schooners were adequately manned, it was done with hand pumps. Sometimes referred to as using "Norwegian steam," it was back-breaking work, but with enough backs aboard, it was effective enough. However as schooners became less competitive, economies were made, one of which was to reduce crew size to five men or so. This was too few to continuously work the pumps by hand, so steam pumps,

The schooner-barge LIZZIE LAW. In 1908, she went to pieces on the Keweenaw. Built in 1875, she was one of the great old time wind wagons before being cut down. KEN E. THRO

usually powered by a donkey engine were used. When a steam pump failed, it was a serious situation. Such a problem existed on the LIZZIE A. LAW on May 9, 1902.

The LAW was in tow of the steamer MONOHANSETT, both loaded with coal for Duluth, when the line parted in a gale. Undaunted, the schooner made sail and ran on before the storm. Unable to take the heavy punishment she was receiving, she anchored about three miles off shore and just to the west of Au Sable Point.

Sighting the distress signal made by the Au Sable Lightkeeper, the Grand Marais life-saving crew started out for the wreck. Their first try was in the surfboat under the tow of a tug, but the high seas forced them to return. Undaunted, they next loaded the surfboat on a wagon, hitched up a team of horses and headed overland. They struggled about seven miles before the steep sand dunes forced them to stop. At this point they launched the surfboat and pulled hard for the schooner.

After a difficult row of nearly three hours, they finally reached the beleaguered vessel. The LAW was indeed in rough shape. Her hold was filled with over seven feet of water, the sails were blown out and the rigging was thickly sheathed in ice. Removing the schooner's exhausted crew to safety at the lighthouse, the life-savers stood watch over the vessel throughout the long, wild night. At daylight they returned the crew to the schooner and set to work trying to save her. After repairing the critical steam pump, the life-savers took the captain and his family to Grand Marais to secure a tug to tow her into port for more complete repair. However, while they were gone, the MONO-HANSETT found the LAW and towed her to shelter at Grand Island. The schooner would live to sail again.

In October of 1908 the LAW did become a Lake Superior ship-wreck, being wrecked at Traverse Island on the east shore of the Keweenaw Peninsula during another Superior gale.

The LIZZIE A. LAW, built in 1875, was owned by the Hines Lumber Company of Chicago. She was 196 feet in length, 34 feet of beam, and 14 feet in depth and measured 747 gross tons.

REFERENCES:

Annual Report of the United States Life-Saving Service, 1903 (Washington, D.C.: U.S. Government Printing Office), pp. 157-158, 304-305.

Harvey Childs Beeson, *Beeson's Inland Marine Directory* (Chicago: Harvey C. Beeson, 1908), p. 132.

Daily Mining Journal (Marquette, Michigan), May 12, 28, 1902.

Detroit Evening News, May 10, 11, 1902.

Detroit Tribune, August 5, 1889.

Duluth News-Tribune, October 21, 22, 25, 1908.

JAMES B. COLGATE AND BARGE NO. 133

September 21, 1907

During a strong north gale the 308-foot whaleback steamer JAMES B. COLGATE with the 292-foot whaleback barge No. 133 were heading for shelter in the lee of Grand Island when trouble struck. The COLGATE wandered off course and grounded, with the shallower draft barge plowing into her stern. Although the damages were costly, both vessels were recovered with comparatively little effort.

The 308-foot whaleback steamer JAMES B. COLGATE.

KEN E. THRO

The 1,713-ton COLGATE, built in West Superior, Wisconsin by the American Steel Barge Company in 1892, was owned by the Pittsburgh Steamship Company. The steamer was eventually lost to shipwreck on Lake Erie on October 21, 1916.

Whaleback barge No. 133, measuring 1,310 tons, was also built in West Superior by American Steel Barge in 1893 and owned by the Pittsburgh Steamship Company. Like the COLGATE, she also succumbed to loss by shipwreck, foundering in an Atlantic gale south of Fire Island, New York in 1911.

REFERENCES:

Daily Mining Journal (Marquette, Michigan), September 23, 1907.

Wilterding, op. cit., pp. 36, 49, 50.

LAKE FRUGALITY
October 22, 1929

The 251-foot steel barge LAKE FRUGALITY was downbound from Marquette in tow of the tug BARRALLTON when the tow cable parted in a northeast gale. The barge was blown on the beach about four miles west of Au Sable Point, while the tug sheltered safely behind Whitefish Point until the gale abated. The barge was salvaged three days later by the BARRALLTON with the help of a Coast Guard vessel and a local fish tug.

The LAKE FRUGALITY had an interesting history, both before and after her stranding. She was essentially a sister ship to the KIOWA, which just five weeks later would wreck at nearly the same spot with deadly results. Both were "Lakers", products of an emergency shipbuilding program during World War I. Although her basic components had been made during the war, the vessel itself was built in 1920 at Lorain, Ohio. In 1927, her engine was removed and put into another vessel, leaving her a lowly tow barge. After she was lengthened in 1927, re-powered in 1943, sold to a Panama-based concern in 1947, and renamed at least twice, (the last time as EASTERN LUCKY), she ended her days when she foundered in salt water on December 12, 1959 far from the Great Lakes.

The LAKE FRUGALITY ashore above Au Sable.

MARQUETTE MARITIME MUSEUM

REFERENCES:

Reverend Edward J. Dowling, *Know Your Lakers of World War I* (Sault Ste. Marie, Michigan: Marine Publishing Company, 1978), p. 80.

Duluth News-Tribune, October 22-24, 1929.

Michigan State Archives, Lansing, Michigan.

Wells, op. cit., p. 79.

SPARTA
November 5, 1940

The last of the major Pictured Rocks shipwrecks was that of the SPARTA during the night of November 5, 1940. The big steel freighter was steaming east of Grand Island when a vicious 60 mile per hour north gale blew her aground at the west end of Mosquito Beach, about fourteen miles east of Munising. Since the ship was in no immediate danger of sinking, Captain Chester Danielson wisely kept his crew aboard until the gale diminished.

At 7:15 a.m. on November 7, Coast Guardsman Eugene Pasquinelli of the Munising Station sighted a lifeboat coming around Miners Castle. Even though the occupants were rowing, it had a small sail up and to the Coast Guardsman's trained eye, she looked like she was in trouble. Within half an hour the Coast Guardsmen had launched their surfboat and were alongside the strange lifeboat. Bobbing about in the middle of Munising Bay they learned of the wreck of the SPARTA.

After bringing the lifeboat's sixteen occupants to the station, the Coast Guardsmen launched the bigger motor lifeboat and headed for the wreck, arriving alongside her at 10 a.m., after a run of an hour and fifteen minutes. There they rescued 21 additional members of the crew.

At 1 p.m. the Coast Guard crew returned to the SPARTA with the ship's officers and officials of the U.S. Steamboat Inspection Service to allow them to make a detailed examination to assess the chances of salvage. In case they were needed, the Coast Guard Cutters RUSH and OSSIPPI hurried to the scene. The experts concluded that if quick action were taken, they just might get her off. To this end, the big wrecking tug FAVORITE was telegraphed for. The wreckers tried their best, but even after two days of pumping with their giant steam pumps as well as the SPARTA's own pumps, both the tug and a Coast Guard cutter failed to budge her. Threatened by an incoming storm, later to be known as the "Armistice Day Storm," they gave up on November 10.

The big steel steamer SPARTA ashore. Note the Coast Guard 36-foot motor lifeboat alongside. HAMILTON COLLECTION, RUTHERFORD B. HAYES LIBRARY

The SPARTA the following spring. Large blocks of ice are still on the stern and portside forward. Emerson Shelly

During the winter, local residents stripped the wreck of most of the equipment that could easily be removed. This included a lifeboat, wheel, portlights and other small items. Most were never recovered.

Despite the decision to abandon the SPARTA, there would be little rest for the Munising Coast Guard crew. On the night of November 12, they received a message from the Michigan Conservation Department that the 433-foot steamer SINALOA was wrecked near Fayette on northern Lake Michigan. Loading up their gear in the station truck, they left to perform another rescue!

The storm that drove the salvagers off the SPARTA and put the SINALOA on the rocks was one of the worst on the lakes. One Cleveland newspaper stated, "...every ship on Lakes Michigan and Superior that arrived in port ...was damaged in some way." At least 70 sailors were killed and 13 ships lost or stranded.

On April 3, 1941 the Roen Steamship Company purchased the SPARTA for $4,500, "where is, as is." Early in the summer Captain

Roen took the tug JOHN ROEN and barge TRANSPORT to the wreck and went to work. His crew plugged leaks in the tank tops with pine plugs, stuffed mattresses into a large hole in the bottom and used heavy jacks on the bow. All the hard work paid off. By late June the SPARTA was afloat and in Munising Bay for temporary repair. In July Roen towed her to drydock in Manitowoc intending to rebuild her for a return to service. She proved too extensively damaged for her to be economically repaired. But Roen was nothing if not creative. Eventually he had the smashed stern cut off from the forward two-thirds of the vessel which became a graving dock at the Sturgeon Bay Shipbuilding Company. Part of the stern was later used as a breakwater near Fairport, Michigan.

The SPARTA had been built in 1902 at the Lorain yard of the American Shipbuilding Company as the Gilchrist freighter FRANK W. HART, thus making her another former Gilchrist vessel eventually lost! Her dimensions were 380 feet in length, 50 feet in beam, 28 feet in depth and 4,307 gross tons. Sold in 1914 to the National Steamship Company, she was renamed SPARTA in 1929. Up until her encounter with the Pictured Rocks, she had led a comparatively charmed life without serious accident.

REFERENCES:

Duluth News-Tribune, November 9-10, 1940.

Arthur and Lucy Frederickson, *Ships and Shipwrecks in Door County, Wisconsin,* Volume II (Sturgeon Bay, Wisconsin: Door County Publishing Company, 1963), pp. 67-68.

Great Lakes Journal, *(Grand Haven, Michigan), April 1941.*

Log of the Munising Coast Guard Station, November 5-15, 1940. National Archives, Record Group 26.

Log of the Grand Marais Coast Guard Station, November 7, 1940. National Archives, Record Group 26.

Alexander Meakin, *The Story of the Great Lakes Towing Company* (Vermilion, Ohio: Great Lakes Historical Society, 1989), p. 169.

John H. Purves, *Roen Steamship Company, the Way it Was* (1983), pp. 33-34.

Reverend Peter J. Van de Linden, ed., *Great Lakes Ships We Remember* (Cleveland: Freshwater Press, 1979), p. 365.

CHAPTER FOUR

ADDITIONAL ACCIDENTS

OTTER
1829

The OTTER, a 75-ton sloop owned by the North West Company, was one of the first vessels on Lake Superior. Although the exact fate of the OTTER is unknown, at least one source suggests she may have been lost with all hands in a gale off Au Sable in 1829.

REFERENCES:

James L. Carter, *Voyageurs' Harbor* (Grand Marais Michigan: Pilot Press, 1967), p. 66.

Mansfield, op. cit., p. 135.

PLANET
June, 1856

Late in June, 1856 the sidewheel steamer PLANET suffered a mechanical breakdown in the open waters of Lake Superior and drifted helplessly until the steamer LADY ELGIN found her, took her in tow and brought her into Grand Island Harbor. The LADY ELGIN took the offending machinery with her on her trip down the lake and sent it to the engine works in Detroit for repair.

REFERENCE:

Detroit Free Press, June 26, 1856.

AMERICAN REPUBLIC
August 25, 1858

The bark AMERICAN REPUBLIC was caught in a storm on the open lake on August 25, 1858. She survived and limped into Grand Island harbor, leaking, missing her main yard and with her jib and mizzen sails split.

REFERENCE:

Milwaukee Sentinel, August 28, 1858.

NORTH STAR
June 3, 1859

The sidewheel steamer NORTH STAR met a severe gale off the Pictured Rocks and had to jettison over $1000 worth of freight from her deck cargo to stay afloat. She was able to make it to shelter in Grand Island Harbor, although her wheelhouse was battered in by the seas. Only three years later, the NORTH STAR ended her career when she caught fire and burned to the waterline at Cleveland, Ohio.

REFERENCES:

Detroit Daily Advertiser, June 11, 1859

David D. Swayze, *Shipwreck!* (Boyne City, Michigan: Harbor House Publishers, 1992) p. 171

JOHN A. DIX
October, 1866

In late October, 1866 the 144-foot U. S. Revenue Cutter JOHN A. DIX went ashore at Grand Island. The side-wheel steamer managed to get off with only slight damage. Seven years later, the DIX again escaped destruction when it was caught in a November gale. The steamer was able to reach safety behind Whitefish Point, but her consorts, the JUPITER and the SATURN, foundered west of the point with a loss of 15 lives.

REFERENCES:

Donald L. Cannery, *U.S. Coast Guard and Revenue Cutters,* 1790-1935 (Annapolis: U.S. Naval Institute Press, 1935), p. 35.

Detroit Advertiser and Tribune, October 26, November 24, December 19, 1866.

Milwaukee Daily Sentinel, October 24, November 27, 1866.

GEORGE W. HOLT
August 26, 1870

The GEORGE W. HOLT, a 265-ton, two-masted schooner, left Marquette with a cargo of iron ore on August 25, 1870. During a storm the next day, she sprang a leak and was run ashore in Grand Island Harbor to keep her from sinking. She was still in a precarious position, however, being in danger of sliding down the sloping bottom into 50 feet of water. The tug DUDLEY quickly came down from Marquette with a steam pump and pumped her out, then the tug JAY C. MORSE towed her to Cleveland to deliver her cargo. After repairs, the HOLT sailed until 1880, when she ended her days wrecked on Port Austin Reef, Lake Huron.

REFERENCES:

Milwaukee Sentinel, September 1, 10, 1870.

Mining Journal (Marquette, Michigan), August 27, 1870.

Swayze, op. cit., p. 111

PELICAN
November 10, 1873

On November 10, 1873, the 200-foot, three-masted schooner PELICAN was downbound from Duluth in tow of the steamer EGYPTIAN when she went ashore on Sand Point. She was released three weeks later with little damage, but her cargo of grain was lost.

REFERENCE:

Mining Journal (Marquette, Michigan), November 15, 1873.

BAHAMA
October 10, 1875

The schooner BAHAMA was forced ashore on Powell Point, south of Grand Island in heavy weather. She was pulled off October 13 by the steamer IRA CHAFFEE without any significant damage.

REFERENCE:

Mining Journal (Marquette, Michigan), October 16, 1875.

FRED KELLY
November 20, 1875

The schooner FRED KELLY ran aground at Grand Island on November 20, 1875. A tug from Marquette was able to release the vessel with little trouble.

REFERENCE:

Milwaukee Daily Sentinel, November 23, 1875

CITY OF PORT HURON
AND DICTATOR
June 28, 1876

The fog at Au Sable Point claimed two more victims in 1876 when the steamer CITY OF PORT HURON and its consort, the schooner DICTATOR ran aground there on the night of June 28. The tug JAY C. MORSE from Marquette came to their rescue and was able to pull them free, but only after each had jettisoned about 100 tons of ore. The DICTATOR was unharmed, but the CITY OF PORT HURON had damaged her keel and leaked badly until she was able to get to drydock for repairs.

REFERENCES:

Detroit Evening News, June 30, 1876.

Milwaukee Daily Sentinel, July 1, 7, 1876.

VERONA
August, 1877

The schooner-barge VERONA, in tow of the steam barge SPARTA, somehow managed to collide with another tow barge, the SUMATRA, which was in tow of the steamer VIENNA. The accident occurred in the vicinity of Grand Island, and the leaking VERONA was towed into the harbor and allowed to settle in shallow water. She was later raised and returned to service. The SUMATRA also sustained $1000 in damages.

REFERENCES:

Detroit Evening News, August 13, 24, 1877.

Mining Journal (Marquette, Michigan), August 18, 1877.

GENERAL FRANZ SIGEL
1882

The GENERAL FRANZ SIGEL, a three-masted schooner, went ashore at Au Sable Point. The vessel was pulled free with $1000 in damages. The SIGEL's career spanned 40 years, from her launch at Black River, Ohio in 1863 to her demise at Monroe, Michigan in 1903.

REFERENCES:

Swayze, op. cit., p. 217

Wells, op. cit., p. 13.

SOUTHWEST
1882

In 1882, the schooner SOUTHWEST was downbound with iron ore when she sprung a leak and was run aground in shallow water near Grand Island. She was later recovered and repaired at a cost of $3500. In 1898 the SOUTHWEST became a total loss when she struck the rocks of the Huron Islands and sank in 100 feet of water.

REFERENCE:

Wells, op. cit., p. 13.

GEORGE SHERMAN
October 10, 1883

The GEORGE SHERMAN, a three-masted schooner, stranded on the east side of Grand Island with minor damages. She was pumped out a few days later. In 1887 the SHERMAN would be lost in a major shipwreck at Shot Point, ten miles east of Marquette.

REFERENCE:

Wells, op. cit., p. 14.

The GEORGE SHERMAN stranded briefly at Grand Island.
DANIEL R. FOUNTAIN

GLASGOW
August, 1884

The steam barge GLASGOW was upbound with a coal cargo for Duluth when a northwest squall forced her ashore at Grand Island. She had been trying to come in under the lee of the island's south point for shelter but took the island a bit too close. After jettisoning 75 tons of cargo and with the help of Captain Everett and the tug DUDLEY, the steamer was released.

REFERENCE:

Mining Journal (Marquette, Michigan), August 16, 1884.

OUDOTTE SAILBOAT
October 17, 1887

Small craft were often the victims of Lake Superior's fury. One such vessel was a sailboat owned by John Oudotte of Marquette. She left the city with a crew of three and a cargo of supplies intended for Johnson's Mill near the Rock River. The sailboat was last sighted at 10 a.m. Tuesday by the lightkeeper at Grand Island North Light. The boat appeared to be light, so the keeper thought that it was on the return trip, but it apparently never arrived in Marquette.

REFERENCE:

Mining Journal (Marquette, Michigan), October 22, 1887.

UNNAMED FISHING TUG
November 9, 1894

Unnamed fish tug, wrecked near Powell Point.

SAILING YACHT
May 28, 1895

A dismasted sailing yacht was picked up by the schooner CRISS GROVER near Grand Island. There was no sign of life in the vicinity, but it was assumed that the yacht belonged to one of several camping and fishing parties known to be in the area.

REFERENCE:

Detroit Evening News, May 31, 1895.

P.B. LOCKE
August 31, 1895

The schooner P.B. LOCKE was downbound with a cargo of sandstone from Portage Entry when she got caught in a heavy northwester and began to leak. Her master, Captain H. Durand, ran her for shelter in the lee of Grand Island, where she filled with water and sank in shallow water. She was pumped out a few days later and, with a steam pump on board to keep her dry, sailed for Toledo where she received $1800 worth of repairs. The LOCKE's end came in 1912 when she foundered in Lake Ontario off Port Hope, Ontario.

REFERENCES:

Daily Mining Journal (Marquette, Michigan), September 2, 1895.

Detroit Evening News, September 2, 7, 20, 1895.

Swayze, op. cit., p. 135

VOLUNTEER
July 15, 1896

The VOLUNTEER was a large barge used by Alger Smith & Company to haul supplies to its lumber camps along the lake. On July 15, 1896, she went ashore four miles west of Au Sable Point.

REFERENCES:

Alger County Republican (Munising, Michigan), October 27, 1893.

Labadie. op. cit., p. 167

M.M. DRAKE
October 21, 1896

The steamer M.M. DRAKE stranded in Munising's east channel in a heavy snowstorm on the morning of October 21, 1896. The schooner CRISS GROVER came from Marquette and lightered part of her cargo of ore, allowing her to be released. The steamer later sank off Vermilion Point on October 2, 1901.

REFERENCES:

Daily Mining Journal (Marquette, Michigan), October 22, 24, 1896.

Detroit Evening News, October 21, 1896.

GEORGE PRESLEY
October 22, 1896

The sand spit in the west channel to Grand Island Harbor proved troublesome for the GEORGE PRESLEY when the schooner went aground there on October 22, 1896. She was released with little difficulty after being lightered by the schooner CRISS GROVER. Nine years later, the PRESLEY was destroyed when it ran aground and caught fire at Washington Harbor, Wisconsin.

REFERENCES:

Daily Mining Journal (Marquette, Michigan), October 24, 1896.

Detroit Evening News, October 23, 1896.

Swayze, op. cit., p. 192

CONNELLY BROTHERS
November 12, 1901

The 210-foot schooner-barge CONNELLY BROTHERS, coal laden, dragged her anchors during a storm and was driven ashore at Sand Point. The steamer ZILLAH and the small tugs LAURA and HICKLER attempted to pull her free but were unsuccessful. When it was feared the schooner would go to pieces in the storm, the crew was removed by small boat. The following day the powerful tug SCHENCK arrived from Marquette and pulled the schooner free without damage.

REFERENCES:

Daily Mining Journal (Marquette, Michigan), November 13, 15, 1901.

Detroit Evening News, November 13, 1901.

Duluth News-Tribune, November 13-15, 1901.

CARTAGENA
September 20, 1904

The steamer CARTAGENA was upbound for Marquette with 2300 tons of coal when she was forced to seek shelter from a northeast gale in Grand Island Harbor. In the dark of night, she went aground near the south shore of the island, but was pulled off with little damage the next afternoon by the tug SILVER SPRAY.

REFERENCES:

Daily Mining Journal (Marquette, Michigan), September 26, 1904.

The Munising News, September 23, 1904.

MARITANA
September 18, 1905

The 340-foot steel steamer MARITANA, caught in a screaming norther, sustained $15,000 in damages after scraping a Grand Island Reef.

REFERENCE:

Wells, op. cit., p. 35.

Caught in the maw of a north gale, the MARITANA bottomed out on a Grand Island reef. KEN E. THRO

PORTAGE
November 21, 1905

The 1,608-ton wooden steamer PORTAGE of Cleveland ran off course and went aground near Au Sable Reef. The Grand Marais life-savers and hired laborers worked for two days jettisoning 500 tons of her cargo of salt before she could be eased off the reef.

REFERENCES:

Carter, op. cit., p. 66.

Daily Mining Journal (Marquette, Michigan), November 23, 1905

Detroit Evening News, November 21, 22, 1905.

Mining Journal (Marquette, Michigan), November 25, 1905.

CATIGEE
1910

In 1910 the wooden steamer CATIGEE survived a northwest blow only by jettisoning 40 horses from her cargo to lighten ship.

ZENITH CITY
July 26, 1910

Another victim of the Au Sable fog was the 388-foot, 3,850-ton ZENITH CITY. Downbound from Marquette with iron ore, the large steel steamer plowed into the reef about one mile off shore. She was pulled off without trouble but needed several new bottom plates. Damages totaled $10,000.

The steel steamer ZENITH CITY, briefly a victim of the Au Sable fogs.
KEN E. THRO

The ZENITH CITY was built in 1895 at the Chicago Shipbuilding Company for the American Steamship Company. When launched, she was one of the longest vessels on the Great Lakes. The ZENITH CITY was scrapped at Hamilton, Ontario in 1947.

REFERENCES:

Annual Report of the United States Life-Saving Service (Washington, D.C.: Government Printing Office, 1911), p. 128.

Detroit Evening News, July 29, 1910

Mining Journal (Marquette, Michigan), August 20, 1910.

Van der Linden, op. cit., p. 404.

PILE DRIVER
November 24, 1912

The same storm that sank the steamer SOUTH SHORE also toppled a pile driver off a scow into Munising harbor.

CARLOTTA
1913

The gasoline powered motorboat CARLOTTA was lost off Grand Island as the result of a fire. No lives were lost.

D.R. VAN ALLEN
November, 1913

The steamer D.R. VAN ALLEN, a Canadian lumber hooker, lost several tons of hay during a storm and was forced to anchor in Munising Bay for shelter and repairs.

WYOMING
October 11, 1914

Bound up in ballast for Duluth, the wooden steamer WYOMING steamed into a strong northwester when passing Au Sable Point. In an attempt to turn and run before the storm for shelter, she fell off into the trough of the sea. Before she managed to claw her way back on course, she broke the main straps and fastenings to the hull and opened the topsides and deck amidships. In all the steamer received storm damages of $5000, a considerable sum in 1914 for a vessel that never actually "wrecked."

REFERENCE:

Wells, op. cit., p. 54.

In October 1914, the WYOMING received heavy storm damage off Au Sable Point.　　　　　KEN E. THRO

ROTARIAN
September 21, 1923

On September 21, 1923 the ROTARIAN, a 147-foot wooden passenger steamer experienced engine trouble near Grand Island and required a major rebuild.

ALICE L.
August 30, 1929

The gas fish tug ALICE L. foundered east of Au Sable Point with the loss of one life.

ARVILLA CW
October 23, 1929

Tug ARVILLA CW stranded on Powell Point and went to pieces during a storm.

GEORGIAN
November 28, 1932

The GEORGIAN, a 247-foot Canadian package freighter, ran aground on a reef near Trout Point on Grand Island while running for shelter. She was recovered May 29, 1933 by the wrecking steamer MAPLECOURT with only slight damage.

The Canadian steamer GEORGIAN photographed during the opening of the Welland Canal. DOWLING COLLECTION

GLADIATOR AND DERRICK BARGE NO. 8
October 11, 1933

On October 11, 1933, the tug GLADIATOR and derrick barge No. 8 with a tow of 35 pontoons and dredge discharge pipe ran into heavy weather off Pictured Rocks resulting in the scow and the entire string going ashore at Au Sable Point. The tug, barge and most of the pontoons were recovered.

MINERS CASTLE
August 31, 1941

The fish tug MINERS CASTLE sank in a storm somewhere in the vicinity of Grand Portal with four men aboard.

REFERENCE:

Labadie, op. cit, p. 173.

MARYMAID
1943

The MARYMAID, a small fishing craft, foundered off Munising.

ROAMER
July 3, 1949

The 30-foot charter fishing boat ROAMER was swamped during a sudden squall east of Wood Island, throwing nine men into the stormy waters. One died from an apparent heart attack, but others were picked up about two hours later by a search party from Munising.

REFERENCE:

Labadie, op. cit, p. 173.

FISHING BOAT
1959

A small 20-foot vessel was lost in the west channel during a north squall drowning three fishermen.

FISHING BOAT
1973

A fishing boat was lost off Five Mile Point when swamped by heavy seas. There was no loss of life.

CHAPTER FIVE

PICTURED ROCKS MYSTERIES

The Pictured Rocks have been a landmark since the beginning of navigation on Lake Superior, and Grand Island has served as a harbor of refuge for Indians, fur traders, missionaries, miners and sailors throughout history. Their stories have been well documented, so it might seem that all the details of the area's maritime past would be known. Nonetheless, numerous mysteries remain.

Of the 30 ships known to have been total losses near the Pictured Rocks, nearly half remain undiscovered to this day. Some vessels such as the MERCHANT were only assumed to have been lost in the area, and could be anywhere on the bottom of the lake. Others were stranded in shallow, exposed locations and were battered to pieces by Superior's storms and ice. Traces might yet be found of these vessels, including the ONEIDA CHIEF, UNION, and ANNIE COLEMAN near Au Sable Point, the CRUISER at Chapel Beach, the ALTA near Trout Bay, and the MARQUETTE on the mainland side of the west channel.

Probably most fascinating to the wreck hunter is the possibility of finding a vessel lying intact on the lake bottom in depths accessible to divers. The ORIOLE was sunk by collision an unknown distance off Grand Island, the EMMA A. MAYES sank seven miles northwest of the island, the CULLIGAN in the same general area, and the MICHI-

GAN 20 miles to the east. Although a quick look at a chart of the area of these wrecks shows water 700 feet or deeper, there are also shallower reefs and sand banks within sport diving depth in the same areas. Closer to shore, the tug WOOD ISLAND reportedly sank in a mere 60 feet of water a mile and a half off Fivemile Point. Given the increased availability of remote sensing technology such as sidescan sonar and the wider use of video depthfinders by boaters, some of these undiscovered wrecks might well join the list of dive sites along the Pictured Rocks.

On the other side of the coin, there are other discovered shipwrecks in Pictured Rocks waters whose identities are unknown. During the inaugural season of Grand Island Charters' glass-bottom boat tours, passengers and crew spotted some previously undiscovered wooden wreckage close to shore along Grand Island's "Thumb." The wreckage consisted of a section of a schooner's bottom about 150 feet long by 35 feet wide along with a part of a side 130 feet long and 15 feet deep. At first the wooden hull pieces were thought to be the remains of the schooner ALTA, which went ashore somewhere near Trout Bay in 1905. Closer examination showed the wreckage to be that of a scow schooner rather than the conventionally-constructed ALTA. A scow schooner was a cheaply built vessel with a flat bottom, flat sides and a square bow and stern. Historical research has failed to produce any record of a scow schooner meeting its end anywhere near Grand Island.

The sandy shallows extending north from Sand Point hold the remains of several wrecked ships. Some of the wreckage can be attributed to the heavily-built steamer MICHAEL GROH. Two schooner hulls located near the point pose more of a riddle. In his Submerged Cultural Resources Study, Pictured Rocks National Lakeshore, historian C. Patrick Labadie concludes that the western wreck is most probably the MARY M. SCOTT, but offers no suggestion as to the identity of the other hulk. The mystery schooner is often totally buried in sand, only occasionally becoming exposed. From what little can be seen of the wreck, it appears to have been a three-masted "canal" schooner, that is, one built to a maximum size of 145 feet long by 26 feet wide in order to fit through the Welland Canal between Lake Erie and Lake Ontario. Traces of her cargo of iron ore lie buried in her hull. Part of the deck of a schooner with its wooden anchor windlass lies buried in sand a few hundred yards away and may be part of the same wreck. On one occasion when the shifting sand revealed a large section of the hull, divers found an iron casting, possibly part of the steering gear, which was marked "Tallcot & Underhill Oswego NY." This might suggest (but hardly proves) that the vessel was built there. The schooner remains unidentified.

During the heyday of the Upper Peninsula's logging industry, huge rafts of pine logs were routinely towed across Lake Superior from the timber-producing forests to sawmills along the shore. These "rafts" were nothing more than floating logs corralled inside a log boom and towed by a tug or steamer. The log boom consisted of immense white pine logs which were chained end to end into a string several hundred yards long. The towing steamer would make fast to one end of the boom and tow it in a circle around a mass of floating logs until it came to the tail end of the boom. With both ends of the boom made fast to the tug's towing bitts, the boat would slowly steam off toward the mill, towing thousands of board feet of timber behind it.

This system worked beautifully in calm weather, but storms could wreak havoc on the rafts. In high waves, some of the logs could be washed out of the boom, and in the worst conditions the booms might part, releasing thousands of logs to drift about in the lake. After the storms subsided, these wayward logs would be rounded up and re-formed into rafts, but some always escaped and either drifted ashore or became waterlogged and sank.

Long after the vast stands of virgin pine in the Upper Peninsula had fallen to the logger's saw, it was discovered that these sunken logs were still solid, marketable timber despite their years underwater. During the 1950's, a hard-hat diver named Schumacher is said to have worked at salvaging some of these logs which had washed in and sunk in the waters around Munising. Schumacher worked from a wooden barge equipped with a steam-powered hoist. Walking along the bottom in his heavy copper helmet, canvas and rubber suit, and lead-soled boots, the diver would fasten a cable to the submerged logs and an assistant on the barge would winch them aboard.

When Schumacher's underwater logging days came to an end, his barge was stripped and abandoned in Grand Island's Murray Bay. Today the boiler from the barge's donkey steam engine can be seen standing out of a few feet of water inside Muskrat Point. The barge is rumored to lie in shallow water a short distance to the east.

Beyond the realm of historical fact and physical evidence, rumors, legends and stories of shipwrecks abound in the Grand Island area. An early example of these ephemeral vessels is the supposed discovery of the MERCHANT. In 1889, some 42 years after the wreck, Peter White reported, "I have ascertained that on her way up she sprang a leak and sank off Grand Island, about four miles out, in 70 fathoms of water. Passengers and crew are still in her hull and it is in fairly good order, at least this was the case when I looked at her in her last resting place a year or so since." White admitted, however, that his detailed knowledge had come to him in a dream. Another party claimed to have spotted the tops of the schooner's masts some 30 feet below the lake's surface five years after it disappeared, but the MERCHANT remains undiscovered to this day.

With the advent of sport scuba diving, stories of lost and "secret" wrecks grew. Some of the more fantastic rumors, such as the schooner said to lie in 60 feet of water in the west channel with its sails still set, can be discounted as no more than divers' yarns. Others may have some basis in fact. A dive shop operator in Christmas used to tell of a diver who would anchor and dive in the same spot between Williams Island and Grand Island. The diver claimed to be diving on a wreck, but would never take anyone else with him. He dove there for several years before being killed in an automobile accident, taking his secret to his grave. Nobody has ever been able to relocate this "secret" wreck.

There are several other rumors of shipwrecks in the area. Off Wood Island, fisherman have reported snagging their nets on something on the bottom, and others have seen unusual shapes on their depthfinders which they believed to be the masts of a sunken vessel. Another schooner is reputed to lie offshore from Miners Castle, hidden in a lake-bottom canyon and nearly invisible to depthfinders.

During the early 1980's, some shipwreck hunters became excited when their depthfinder showed what appeared to be masts standing up off the bottom in 160 feet of water near Miners Castle. Gearing up with double tanks, the divers started down on their deep dive with high expectations of dropping onto a shipwreck standing intact on the bottom. Instead of masts, however, they found themselves among several tall trees standing upright on the lake bottom! One possible explanation for the "sunken forest" is that the trees eroded and fell from the cliffs of the Pictured Rocks, drifted out to deep water and sank roots-first.

Another fascinating possibility is that thousands of years ago when the lake level was lower, the trees actually grew where they now stand. A parallel might be drawn with the Gribben Forest, a stand of 10,000 year-old spruce trees uncovered during the excavation of a tailings basin for the Tilden Mine in Marquette County. Some of the Gribben trees were still standing where they had grown and had been buried by sand and silt washed out from a melting glacier at the end of the last Ice Age. During the Ice Age, the Great Lakes as well as the oceans were believed to have been much lower than present levels due to the tremendous amount of water frozen in the glaciers that covered much of the continents. The trees off Miners Castle might have grown on the shores of a smaller, shallower Lake Superior and drowned when the lake level rose with the melting of the glaciers.

Another mysterious tree was found amid the wreckage of the wooden freighter HERMAN H. HETTLER in Munising's east channel. Suspecting that the tree was extremely old, charter boat captain Pete Lindquist of Munising sent samples of the wood for carbon dating. The laboratory results showed an age of 7910 years, plus or minus 100 years, but provided no clue as to why a nearly 8000 year old tree would be found amid the remains of a 1926 shipwreck.

The wreck of the KIOWA is the site of another riddle. A large framing member from a wooden vessel was found among the steamer's steel wreckage. It must have been carried to the site by strong storm-born currents or winter's ice, but its source is unknown. Ice movements, storm currents, and wreckage movement are almost invariably west to east on the south shore of Lake Superior, but there are no known wooden wrecks within ten miles to the west of the KIOWA. Perhaps an undiscovered wreck lies hidden on the lake bottom somewhere up-current.

CHAPTER SIX

THE LIGHTHOUSES

GENERAL

The lighthouses gracing the Pictured Rocks are an integral part of the story of the area's maritime past. To gain a full understanding of this record, the reader must have some comprehension of the history of the lights, as well as a general appreciation of the lighthouses on the Great Lakes.

Government's involvement in safe navigation began early in American history. The first lighthouse was established on the east coast in 1716 at Little Brewster Island at the entrance to Boston Harbor. By 1789, there were a dozen active beacons.

On the Great Lakes, the first light reportedly was established in 1815 at Fort Niagara on Lake Ontario, although there is some debate about this in historical circles. It is possible the Presque Isle Light on Lake Erie may have preceded it.

As commerce grew on the lakes, the number of lighthouses increased. By 1865 there were seven on Lake Ontario, a dozen on Lake Huron, 26 on Lake Michigan and 15 on Lake Superior. Each new light improved safety by warning mariners of dangerous shores and reefs as well as guiding them to sheltered harbors.

Lake Superior received its first light in 1849, although there is some confusion whether it was at Copper Harbor or at Whitefish Point since records indicate both were established at the same time. Other Lake Superior lights quickly followed: Eagle Harbor in 1851, Raspberry Island in 1852, Marquette in 1855, Grand Island North in 1856, Keweenaw Bay in 1856, Gull Rock in 1867, Grand Island East Channel in 1869 and Au Sable Point in 1874.

ORGANIZATION

Originally all lights were under the auspices of the fifth auditor of the Treasury Department. While significant growth occurred during this period, overall management was poor. The attempt was generally to spend the least possible amount of money without regard to securing acceptable equipment or results. The outcome was a rising chorus of complaints from sailors, ship owners and insurers. In 1851 Congress directed the Secretary of the Treasury to convene a special board to investigate the situation. The board's report was thorough and inclusive, and concluded that the lighthouse establishment was poorly managed in both economy and efficiency, keepers were ill-trained and in many cases incompetent, and the lamps and reflectors were obsolete and inferior in design.

Responding to the investigation, Congress in 1852 established a nine member Lighthouse Board with the Secretary of the Treasury as ex-officio president. Other members included scientists, U.S. Army engineers, U.S. Navy officers and members of the U.S. Coast Survey. The new Board organized the lights into districts. The Great Lakes were initially divided into the Tenth and Eleventh Districts. A reorganization in 1886 resulted in the Tenth District consisting of Lakes Erie and Ontario; the Ninth District, Lake Michigan; and the Eleventh, Lakes Superior and Huron.

The Board also appointed an inspector for each district, giving him the responsibility of building and maintaining the lights and equipment as well as buying supplies. The inspector was required to inspect each station in the district every three months. As the number of lights increased, additional help was provided for the inspector. An Army Corps of Engineers officer assisted with construction and maintenance duties. Local collectors of customs were kept on as lighthouse superintendents. They had the responsibility of appointing and paying keepers and handling routine fund disbursements. Eventually their role was phased out completely.

Central depots for forwarding supplies and performing repairs to the apparatus were also established. On the lakes they were at one time or another located at Detroit, St. Joseph and Milwaukee.

Improvements under the Board's leadership were significant. They established lights where needed and made certain they were well kept and reliable. Inefficient men were fired. The Board also experimented with new technology, trying whatever new equipment or fuels they thought might offer improvement. Prior to the advent of the Board, the U.S. provided the worst lights in the civilized world. Afterwards, we had the best. In 1903, the Board was transferred to the Commerce Department.

Early lightkeepers often were selected based on political loyalties. Trustworthiness, reliability or competence were not requirements; political affiliation was. Congressmen and senators with a light in their district didn't hesitate to use the appointment of a keeper as a real plum for a deserving bootlicker. Although the actual appointment of a keeper was the responsibility of the local collector of customs, these worthies were relatively far down the political food chain. Depending on the results of an election, wholesale dismissals and appointments were made. This happened so frequently that in the interest of efficiency and economy, the Lighthouse Board had blank forms printed to notify keepers that they had been replaced!

The Lighthouse Board was well aware of the problem and tried its best to minimize the deleterious effect of politics and achieved some limited success. It did establish standards for the keepers to meet, which included a three month probationary period. After being tested on his duties by the district inspector or engineer, he could be dismissed for failure.

It wasn't until 1884 that uniforms were prescribed for keepers. Until then, they dressed to suit their own tastes.

The public outcry against the evils of the spoils system finally resulted in the passage by Congress in 1883 of the Pendleton Civil Service Act. Under it, appointments to key government positions would be based on ability, and special examinations were required of all applicants. Although initially only a few agencies were covered by the act, later presidents gradually increased the number. In 1896 President Cleveland added the U.S. Lighthouse Service and from then on appointments were based on merit. Following World War I however, special consideration was often given to wounded veterans, a most laudable effort on behalf of those who so bravely served.

As times change, so do methods of management and administration, and in 1910 Congress abolished the Lighthouse Board and established in its stead the Bureau of Lighthouses. The new organization remained under the Commerce Department. Instead of the nine member board, there was now only one man, the Commissioner of Lighthouses.

The new commissioner had the authority to organize not more than 19 districts, each to be headed by a civilian inspector. An Army Corps of Engineers officer assigned to each district continued the role of providing professional expertise to lighthouse design, construction and maintenance. The entire organization was firmly under civilian control and leadership.

Growth was phenomenal. Nation wide, in 1910 there were 11,713 aids of all types. Within three years there were 12,824 including 1,462 lights and 51 light ships.

As in the old U.S. Life-Saving Service, a viable retirement system was slow in coming. The life-savers finally got theirs in 1915 when they merged with the U.S. Revenue-Marine to form the Coast Guard. Three years later the lighthouse men got theirs.

On July 7, 1939, in another move for greater governmental efficiency, the president abolished the old Bureau of Lighthouses and transferred its duties to the Coast Guard. The Coast Guard operated under the Treasury Department, so lighthouses which had started under the Treasury Department had now returned.

As part of the process of integrating into the Coast Guard, lighthouse personnel were given the option of either retaining their civilian status or converting to a military position. About half chose to convert.

CONSTRUCTION

Most Great Lakes lighthouses were built during a relatively short period and are generally similar in construction. To withstand the ravages of storms, the lights were well constructed of brick or stone. Wood may have been used for mere range lights, but never for "real" lights. They tended to be square in shape and plain in design with no emphasis placed on anything "frivolous." The lights were not usually "one of a kind," but built from standard plans and designs. For example the Au Sable Light, eight miles east of Grand Marais and the Outer Island Light in the Apostle Islands were both built in 1874 from the same plans. In many instances, however, the basic design was modified to meet a particular site requirement.

Usually the light station would consist of a compound of several buildings: the lighthouse proper, a combination tower and dwelling, an oil house and a fog signal house. A pier or dock was also built to facilitate the landing of personnel and supplies.

LAMPS, LENSES AND LIGHTS

The earliest lights on the Great Lakes used Argand lamps with parabolic reflectors. These lamps were complicated, inefficient and difficult to maintain.

Between 1852-59, nearly all of the Great Lakes lights were given the new Fresnel lens. This lens has a powerful central lamp surrounded by refracting prisms and glass rings. The rings and prisms bend and guide the light, aiming it outward in powerful beams. Invented in 1820, the lens was named for Augustin Fresnel, a French scientist.

Fresnel lenses were classified into seven sizes or orders, relating to their power. A sixth order lens was less than a foot in diameter, while the largest lens, a first order was six feet in diameter and nearly 12 feet high. The lenses were also very expensive, a factor which discouraged their early adoption by the United States. Eventually, the United States shifted to the Fresnel system and realized that as a result of their efficiency in reducing fuel costs, using only a quarter of previous requirements, they soon paid for themselves.

Up until about 1864, the Great Lakes lights, as well as all others, burned sperm whale oil. When its price increased to a level the government thought too high, the fuel was switched initially to a lard oil and later to kerosene or as it was then called, mineral oil. The ultimate improvement was made in 1904 when the service changed to the use of incandescent oil vapor lamps. Operating much like a Coleman lantern, fuel is forced into a vaporizer chamber and then into a mantle. This arrangement increased brilliance manyfold over the old-fashioned wicks. Today all lights are electric powered.

FOG SIGNALS

og signals were also maintained at many lights. At first they were only hand-rung bells, but by 1851 mechanically operated systems were in use. Later steam whistles and sirens were used. By 1900 nearly all fog signals were of the steam powered variety. One problem with the steam whistle, however, was the long time needed to raise the necessary steam pressure before the signal could sound. Often the process of starting a boiler fire and waiting patiently for the steam pressure to rise to a sufficient level could take as long as 45 minutes. In a busy channel this was a very long time indeed. Eventually steam signals were replaced with ones using compressed air which greatly decreased response time. The compressed air was provided by gasoline or diesel engines driving special air compressors and was stored in large tanks for instant use.

DAILY ROUTINE

unning a light took a special kind of person. The daily routine was difficult and demanding. It also was tedious and boring, depending on one's outlook. The light had to be maintained in a constant state of readiness. The lens had to be cleaned and polished, the lamp filled and wicks trimmed and all associated apparatus kept in functioning order. It is from the work of trimming the wick that the old keepers received the nickname "wickies." Regulations called for the light to be ready for the night's use not later than 10 a.m. The grounds as well as all buildings and facilities also had to be kept clean and orderly.

The exact details of the keeper's responsibilities could be found in the publication *Instructions to Light-Keepers* provided by the Lighthouse Board. Literally everything he needed to know was spelled out in laborious precision.

To help pass the time and also provide fresh vegetables, keepers usually kept small gardens. Often they were not very successful since the lights were usually located in areas that did not have good soil. In some instances keepers brought boxes of their own garden soil with them. For many years this was the practice of the keeper at Stannard Rock Light. Located 44 miles out in Lake Superior, almost directly north of Marquette, the light is often lashed by terrific storms. As a result the keeper repeatedly "lost" his gardens to the grasping waves.

To help fight the boredom the Lighthouse Service also provided special portable libraries. Packed into sets of roughly 50 books, each library box could easily be exchanged between stations. As an added bonus, the boxes were designed to stack into neat book shelves, thus helping to minimize furniture requirements.

The lights were resupplied by special vessels called lighthouse tenders. These tough little vessels carried not only all the operating stores needed by the lights but also the dreaded inspector. These men were infamous for their "white glove" examinations of stations. A poor inspection could spell the end of a keeper's career.

Some keepers handled the deadly daily routine well. Others however, after a careful reading of their daily logs, appeared to "lose their marbles." More than one keeper was driven over the edge of sanity by the terrible grinding isolation and lack of human contact.

A lighthouse was often a family enterprise where the husband and wife teamed up to make the light a success. The husband as keeper assumed full responsibility for the light proper, while the wife took charge of the dwelling.

Lighthouse inspectors often used this team effort to their advantage. After carefully examining the husband's light, he would pull the man aside and say something to the effect that he was doing a fine job but that his wife was letting him down. She just wasn't keeping the quarters up to standard. Perhaps the keeper could encourage her to do a better job. When he finished checking the quarters, the inspector would pull the wife aside and tell her the same thing about the husband's performance.

AU SABLE LIGHT

The most famous of the Pictured Rocks lights is that at Au Sable Point. The point was recognized as a hazard to navigation at least as early as the 1660's when Pierre Esprit Radisson called it "...most dangerous when there are any storms." As lake traffic boomed in the middle of the nineteenth century with the discovery of iron ore and the opening of the Soo canal, Au Sable Point reef, reaching out into presumably safe waters, was especially dangerous. Unless warned off, vessels could fall prey to this ship trap, breaking their hulls on the unforgiving Jacobsville sandstone.

The region was also infamous for the thick fogs caused by the interaction of cool lake air with warmer currents rising from the Grand Sable dunes. Long recognizing the dangers of the area, shipping companies, as well as others, began to lobby for a light. For example, the

Au Sable Point Light as viewed from the west.
FREDERICK STONEHOUSE

The original keeper's house is on the left. The new house is on the right.
DONALD L. NELSON

Marquette Mining Journal, said on July 29, 1871 that, "...in all navigation of Lake Superior, there is none more dreaded by the mariner than from Whitefish Point to Grand Island." The Eleventh Lighthouse District, in whose purview the new light lay, commented in its annual report that a light was more needed at Au Sable Point than any other unprotected location in the district.

Originally Au Sable Point had been known as Point Aux Sables by the French, who named it for the nearby dunes. When the new Americans assumed control over the region, the name was translated to "Big Sable Point," which caused confusion with Big Sable Point on Lake Michigan. To end the chaos, in 1910 the Lighthouse Service officially renamed it Au Sable Light.

In 1872 Congress appropriated $40,000 to build a lighthouse at the point. The State of Michigan deeded 326 acres land to the federal government for the light station. Construction started the following year and on August 19, 1874 the light officially went into service. Its flickering and comparatively weak kerosene flame was multiplied to 6,750 candlepower after being reflected by 90-degree mirrors through a 270-degree Fresnel lens. The steady beam cut clearly 17 3/4 miles out into the black night. A hand-cranked foghorn was also installed to warn vessels off in thick weather.

The brick tower stands a full 86 feet high. Its base is 16 feet, six inches in diameter and the top, 12 feet, eight inches. The 23-foot foundation of rubble masonry rests firmly on bedrock. A passageway connects the tower to the keeper's residence. Au Sable Point Light was not unique in design; in fact, it is identical to the lighthouse at Outer Island in western Lake Superior, also placed in operation in 1874.

Duty at Au Sable was lonely for both the keepers and their families. It was considered one of the most isolated mainland lights in the country. The nearest village was Grand Marais, 12 miles to the east, via a narrow path running along the base of the steep dunes. During stormy weather the trail was virtually impassable due to the crashing waves. Usually all personnel and supplies came to the light by boat, coming ashore at a small pier at the base of the station. Travel in winter was by snowshoes, sleds and dog teams.

By regulation keepers were required to keep journals, faithfully recording daily events and activities. These documents provide a fascinating look into the human history of this isolated station, since they recorded news of the keeper's families, the arrival of the lighthouse tenders, daily chores, visitors and even the excitement of shipwrecks.

Keeper Napoleon Beedon described on December 8, 1876 a "...light brees," from the south, that by 5 p.m. had been replaced by a "...frightful storm" that blew down 50 trees or more close by the lighthouse and caused him to fear that "...the lighthouse and tower would be blow down as they shook like a leaf the wind was N.N. West snowing and freesing it was the worst storm I ever saw on Lake Superior."

On September 25, 1883, Frederick W. Boesler Sr., the keeper who took over from Beedon in 1879, wrote that the weather was "...clear,

A Lothrop hand-powered foghorn as originally used at Au Sable.
Donald L. Nelson

blowing hard from the northwest," as he watched the stranded steamer MARY JARECKI, on the reef since the previous July, beaten to splinters before his eyes.

Keeper Gus Gigandet, who arrived on May 21, 1884 with his wife and an assistant keeper, noted in his journal that, "I feel contented and satisfied with the station." Gigandet's feeling must have indeed run deep since he remained keeper until his death on October 29, 1896. Bad storms were a frequent companion. On November 5, 1886 he recorded "...one of the heaviest gales from the northwest with a blinding snowstorm I have ever experienced." The following July the wind blew so strong that it caused "the tower to shake hard." On July 24, 1893, during the height of a smashing thunderstorm, lightning struck the tower, "burning two holes in the bottom of the tower, right at the foot of the stairs."

While monotony was a constant companion, there were advantages to living at the light. Hunting and fishing were excellent and could always be depended on to supplement the larder. In 1900, Gigandet bragged that he caught 144 brook trout. The journal recorded that on November 4, 1901 the assistant keeper killed a bear so large that it required most of a day for two men to drag it back to the light. The local bears could be very dangerous. A bear at Point Iroquois Light on Whitefish Bay had once dragged a small girl into the woods and devoured her. One assistant, William Laviate, earned extra income by spending his winter working in a local lumber camp. On a horticultural note, in 1881 keeper Boesler wrote that he had "...grafted 24 fruit trees, 12 cherry and 12 of apples." The fruit provided an important supplement to the food supply.

As time passed, many more improvements and additions were made to the station. A wooden boathouse and wood shed in 1875; a brick oil house in 1895; the steam powered fog horn in 1897, as well as piping to carry in lake water to operate the system, replacing the hand cranked unit. However, the first fog signal didn't work and it was a year before a replacement unit was operational, finally ending the keeper's arduous job of cranking the signal when the point was shrouded in fog. Improved boat ways were built in 1901, a new seawall in 1906, the old single story keeper's house was raised to two levels in 1909 and brick privies were added at the same time. A diaphone fog whistle was installed in 1928, the same year a rough road to Grand Marais was finally finished, providing eventual access to the public highway. No longer were the keepers quite so isolated.

During the harsh winters the road was impassable and the isolation complete. The winter seclusion was in part blamed for the deaths of a keeper's son and daughter. Both were buried near the station.

Seeing the station today, nestled into a forest of green trees and other foliage, it is hard to visualize how it looked when it was a working lighthouse. An excellent idea of what the station looked like in 1909 can be drawn from the *Description of Buildings, Premises,*

Equipment, etc. of Au Sable Light Station, by Ralph Tinkerham, Light-House Establishment, Department of Commerce. "The main point on which the light house stands has been cleared of timber for a quarter mile each way from the station to facilitate the visibility of the light to the E'd and W'd. This clearing has grown up to the second growth — small stuff ...Access is by boat or wagon road to within three miles of the station, thence by foot trail; this trail is cleared out so that a team without a load can get to the light station."

The old light was also the scene of personal tragedy for some of the families that maintained it. Keeper Otto Buffe had an especially difficult time. On October 14, 1904 his pregnant wife was very ill and he sent his second assistant to fetch the doctor from Grand Marais. In spite of the physician's best efforts at "4 pm Mrs. Buffe was delivered of a dead male child." The next day the child was lovingly buried on the grounds. In September 1905 another Buffe child died at the light. The next month the Buffe family was transferred to Point Iroquois, away from Au Sable's numbing isolation and tragic memories.

As the 20th century grew older, life at the station gradually improved. A good road was finally built to the station in 1943, making it possible to reach it by car or truck. Batteries were used to power both the light and fog horn then, but electric generators were later installed.

In 1945, the quarters were modernized and the Coast Guard took over from the old civilian keepers. The light itself was automated in 1958, saving an estimated $20,000 a year. On January 12, 1968 Au Sable Light was officially transferred to the National Park Service, although the Coast Guard retained ownership of the light tower and continued its responsibility to maintain the steady beacon that is still as welcome to sailors today as it was in the days of sail.

The original six-foot high third order Fresnel lens, which was produced at a cost of $3,800 and removed in 1957 when the station closed, was returned to the light in 1995. The National Park Service is currently restoring the light to its 1909/1910 appearance.

GRAND ISLAND NORTH LIGHT

Some consider Grand Island to be among the most beautiful islands on the Great Lakes. Roughly eight miles long and three miles wide, it has stark sandstone cliffs the equal of the famous Pictured Rocks, as well as white sandy beaches and small rocky protected coves. Located just north of Munising, its bulk acts as a natural windbreak for Munising Bay. It is also the largest island on the south shore of Superior. The island was a favorite stopping point for early explorers. Pierre Radisson and his brother-in-law Medard Chouart Sieur des Groseilliers were the first Europeans to sight the island and record their experiences in detail, arriving in 1658. A fur trading post was operated on the island for a time in the early 1800's by Astor's American Fur Company. The old North West Company had run a post on the mainland opposite the island in the late 1770's. By 1832 a total of 50 people lived on Grand Island.

In 1840 Abraham Williams arrived and for several generations thereafter he was the major influence. Initially he took over several log cabins abandoned by the American Fur Company. Later Williams and his family operated a sawmill, blacksmith shop and cooperage as well as farming and running a trading post. They also provided cordwood for the many steamers calling at Grand Island harbor. Williams Island, Williams Landing, the Anna River (named for his wife), and Powell Point (for his daughter's husband) are all part of the legacy of this remarkable man.

His family maintained ownership of the island until 1900 when it was sold to the Cleveland Cliffs Iron Company for $93,701.61. The island's timber resource was harvested for many years and for a period the location was used as a corporate retreat and game preserve. For a time the island was stocked with elk, Rocky Mountain sheep, moose, caribou, mule deer and antelope. In spite of problems with local predators, the animal population multiplied and the company used the surplus to stock zoos around the world. To make the island into an exclu-

Grand Island North Light.   FREDERICK STONEHOUSE

sive resort, cabins and lodges as well as horse paths, boats, tennis courts and archery ranges were constructed. The island was promoted as an "ideal summer resort." By 1958 the resort had closed. People had become more interested in other forms of recreation than enjoying the pampered tranquility of the north woods. Later, selected timber was harvested but the island remains undeveloped. The exotic game long since succumbed to the ravages of nature. In 1990 the federal government purchased Grand Island for use as a national recreation area.

The first Grand Island Light was built at the north tip of the island at the edge of a 175-foot cliff. The original light was established in 1856 (some records indicate 1854) as the result of an 1853 appropriation of $5,000 to establish a "lighthouse at Grand Island Harbor." Apparently this structure was made of wood with a 30-foot tower, making it at the time the highest light above sea level on the lakes. This first light didn't last. In 1865 it was reported to be in "wretched condition," due apparently to the inferior materials of original construction.

The light was doubtlessly built in haste, the result of the increasing traffic between the Soo and the iron ore port of Marquette. Grand Island was also the only shelter between these two points and important as a wood stop for the early steamers. The light was needed to safely navigate the coast, especially considering the propensity for coastal sailing.

In 1867 the old light was torn down and a new one built adjacent to it. The new tower stood 40 feet tall with a keeper's house attached. Both were built of brick. A fourth order Fresnel lens comprised the optics. An oil house, storage building and outhouse completed the facility. It continued to be the highest light above sea level on the Great Lakes. To differentiate it from the East Channel Light, it was called North Light, or Grand Island North.

During this same period similar style lights were built at Ontonagon, Gull Rock, Huron Islands and Granite Island. Older lights at Copper Harbor and Marquette were rebuilt to the new North Light design.

North Light sits high above the lake.   FREDERICK STONEHOUSE

Following the SUPERIOR disaster in October 1856, when nine of the survivors made their way there, life at the North Light continued without major interruption, other than on August 5, 1891 when the tower was struck by lightning. In 1941 the keeper was removed and the light changed from oil to acetylene gas. No longer did the trusty old wickie climb the winding tower steps on his rounds. Without the benefit of human habitation, or any significant maintenance, the structure deteriorated greatly. In 1961, the beacon proper was relocated from the stone tower to a pole near the cliff and automated. Also in the 1960s, the property was declared surplus and sold to Dr. Loren Graham, a professor at the Massachusetts Institute of Technology with deep roots in Grand Island. After a great deal of effort, he was able to renovate the building sufficiently to make it his summer home.

North Light was also the scene of a real life murder mystery. What actually happened is still anyone's guess, but the known facts are these:

On June 12, 1908 the body of 30-year old Edward S. Morrison, the assistant lightkeeper at North Light, was discovered in a small sailboat

Edward S. Morrison and his wife Lena.   JO LEE DIBERT-FITKO

near Au Sable Point. Although identification took a while, since few of the local people knew him, it was definite once made. Morrison had a distinctive tattoo of thirteen stars on his left arm, leaving no doubt as to the identity of the remains. Initial reports said his head had been "battered almost beyond recognition" and that "the head and shoulders were fearfully crushed, as if battered by a club." Inexplicably though, a coroner's jury concluded death was due to exposure, thought to be caused by the rough weather on the 7th. Reportedly a second coroner's jury also examined the evidence and returned a verdict that the members were not able to tell how he died, but they had a strong suspicion of murder!

Morrison had been assistant keeper only six weeks when he met his death. A native of Tecumseh, Michigan, he joined the Lighthouse Service on May 1, 1908 and secured the assistant keeper's appointment at North Light. Friends claimed he had a "bright and sunny disposition" and that he "didn't have an enemy in the world."

The keeper of the light was George Genery, a long-time veteran of the Service. Appointed to North Light in 1893, he had been the assistant keeper at Menagerie Island, Isle Royale from 1887 until his posting to Grand Island. It was later claimed he had trouble keeping his assistants since none lasted longer than a season. Working with Genery was said to be difficult at best. The keeper was in Munising on June 6 to get supplies.

Baffled by the discovery of Morrison's body and the knowledge that the beacon had been dark for nearly a week, a delegation from Munising went out to the light. They discovered the supplies Genery had brought back from Munising still piled on the dock. An empty wheelbarrow stood nearby and his coat dangled undisturbed on a hook in the boathouse. Morrison's vest was hanging carefully on the back of a chair, his watch and papers safe in a pocket. Of the three boats normally kept at the station, reports differed whether two or only one was missing. The last official log entry was made on June 5, while the slate entry for the 6th was made in Morrison's hand. Neither gave a clue to anything being amiss. Other than the untended lamp, all else was normal, without evidence of any unusual occurrence. Local volunteers manned the light until the service sent a replacement.

Authorities immediately started a search for the missing keeper, but he had completely dropped out of sight. There were reports that five different men had seen him at various times in Munising between June 9 and 12, and that he was drinking heavily. His wife, living in town, claimed no knowledge of his whereabouts and did not seem overly concerned with his strange disappearance.

There were several theories proffered to explain the case. One said the two men had gone out to lift nets and that Genery had fallen overboard and drowned. Morrison, unfamiliar with a sailboat, then drifted about helplessly until finally perishing from exposure. Friends, however doubted such reasoning. They considered Morrison an expert sailor, and in fact he had previously owned a 32-foot sailboat on the Detroit River.

Another theory is based on their having been paid on the 6th; that they were attacked by one or more unknown assailants on the island, murdered, robbed and the bodies dumped into the sailboats and cast adrift. Morrison's eventually made shore. Genery's never did. Lonely to distraction, no better location for such a crime could be imagined. No one else was in the area to witness such a heinous deed. The nearest neighbor on the island was the Cleveland Cliffs game keeper, whose house was seven miles to the south. There was a story that a body was later discovered in the east channel, but it was apparently never identified so whether it was the missing keeper is unknown. Finding "floaters" was not that unusual, so no definite link between it and Genery was possible.

The third theory was that Morrison was murdered by Genery. It was thought that Morrison had come down to the dock with the wheelbarrow to help carry the supplies back to the light. As evidenced by Genery's coat and Morrison's vest, both men were in shirt sleeves and had likely just finished the hard work of unloading the supplies from the boat. For an unknown reason the two started to argue. Possibly it was the quarrelsome Genery who began by berating Morrison for some failing, real or imagined. In a moment of fury, Genery smashed Morrison's skull with a blunt object, perhaps an oar, shovel or hammer. To hide the dastardly crime, he then placed the body in a sailboat and pushed it out into the lake. With luck it would disappear and after a decent interval he could claim his assistant deserted for no apparent reason. If it was later found, he could claim it must have been a terrible accident, that Morrison left for a sail and evidently fell, injuring his head, or was stuck by the boom during a quick jibe. Regardless, Genery needed a drink, or several, and headed for Munising. Later reconsidering his plan, he went home where he was hidden by his wife. When the body was discovered and the charge "murder" echoed through the town, he fled. Some people claimed he reached Canada were he lived out his days in quiet obscurity.

Perhaps Morrison had a premonition of his own death, or at the very least was very unhappy working for Genery. On June 16, four days after his body was discovered, his wife in Flint received a letter

Assistant lightkeeper Edward S. Morrison's Flint, Michigan headstone.
FREDERICK STONEHOUSE

from him posted just before his death. In it he wrote, "do not be surprised if you hear of my body being found dead along the shore of Lake Superior." He stated Genery was of a "...quarrelsome disposition..." and that he feared "...an accident if he opposed him ..." Did Morrison "oppose" him and did Genery respond to the challenge with murder?

Morrison's death was another example of the old adage, "death always comes in threes." Two years before his sister had been murdered in Toledo. The previous fall a brother was killed when the locomotive he was riding in crashed through a wooden trestle.

Exactly what happened will of course never be known, but it is fair to say that not all men could handle the terrible monotony at the isolated lights. The long empty hours, days, weeks, months and years of crushing sameness could have caused Genery to become more irritable and unbalanced as evidenced by his trouble keeping assistants. Finally, for some unfathomable reason, he snapped resulting in murder most foul and a North Light mystery still unsolved.

EAST CHANNEL LIGHT

The small wooden frame lighthouse on the southeast shore of Grand Island was constructed during the period 1869-1870 for the purpose of guiding vessels into Munising harbor from the east. The land was one of a number of parcels reserved in 1847 for government use. Resembling a small country church in style, its original color was white. The location, opposite the dangerous shoal at Sand Point was critical for safe navigation. By 1905 however, the Lighthouse Board noted that the light was no longer serving its original purpose and, considering difficulties in maintenance and the mariner's desire for improved range lights, its abandonment was only a matter of time. The light was finally abandoned in 1913 as a result of the construction in 1908 of improved range lights. In 1915 the land and lighthouse were privately purchased and divided into lots. The lighthouse building became community property. The building is still privately owned and although it is in badly deteriorated condition, periodic efforts have been made to reinforce the historic structure.

The small light was home to many keepers and their families. The last was George Prior, who served there from 1891 to 1907. Two of his children were born at the light. Difficulties the old keepers had to overcome were many. Just maintaining a reliable and varied food supply was always a problem at the Superior lights and the East Channel Light was no different. Like many other keepers, Prior kept a small garden as well as chickens and perhaps even a cow. Setting a net or two assured fresh fish.

East Channel Light.   DONALD L. NELSON

MUNISING RANGE LIGHTS
WEST CHANNEL

The west channel range lights were established in 1868 to accurately guide vessels clear of the shoal running into the channel west of Grand Island. Vessels entering the bay carefully aligned the rear and front lights to place them on a safe course. The rear range light with a 32-foot tower was identical to the existing East Channel Light. The front range was a 19-foot wooden tower. Each was painted white, as is normal for range markers. Both were lit on August 15, 1868. The present 62-foot conical steel tower was erected in 1914 to replace the original wood structure. It was deactivated in 1969, the same year the front range light was torn down to make room for the Bay Furnace directional light.

West Channel front range light.   FREDERICK STONEHOUSE

West Channel rear range light.   FREDERICK STONEHOUSE

EAST CHANNEL

The east channel range lights, intended to replace the East Channel Light, were erected by the Champion Iron Company of Cleveland in 1908 as the result of a 1907 congressional appropriation of $15,000. The front tower, built of 5/16 inch, riveted steel plates, is 12 feet in diameter at the base, eight feet at the top and 58 feet tall. The rear range light tower, also built of riveted steel, is 10 feet, nine inches at the base, seven feet at the top and 33 feet tall and is located five blocks inland, on the side of a steep hill.

East Channel front range light.   FREDERICK STONEHOUSE

East Channel rear range light. FREDERICK STONEHOUSE

REFERENCES:

Annual Report of the Lighthouse Board, (Washington, D.C.: U.S. Department of the Treasury, various issues).

"Grand Island," Alger County Chamber of Commerce, n.d.

Francis Ross Holland, Jr., *America's Lighthouses, An Illustrated History* (New York: Dover Publications, 1988).

Dr. Loren Graham, correspondence the author, March 9, 1996.

Instructions to Light-Keepers (Allen Park, Michigan: Great Lakes Lighthouse Keepers Association, 1989).

National Maritime Initiative, 1994 Inventory of Historic Light Stations (Washington, D.C.: U.S. Department of the Interior, National Park Service, 1994).

Donald L. Nelson, correspondence to author, March 9, 1996.

Donald L. Nelson, "The Lighthouses of Grand Island on Michigan's Lake Superior." *The Beacon,* December, 1995.

Dennis L. Noble and T. Michael O'Brien, *Sentinels of the Rocks* (Marquette, Michigan: Northern Michigan University Press, 1979).

Grace Lee Nute, *Lake Superior* (New York: Bobbs-Merrill, 1944).

Laurie Penrose, Bill T. Penrose and Ruth Penrose, *A Traveller's Guide to Michigan Lighthouses* (Davison, Michigan: Friede Publications, 1992).

Porcupine Press, August 15-21, 1990.

Faye Swanberg, *"The East Channel Lighthouse,"* Alger County Historical Society, n.d.

CHAPTER SEVEN

MUNISING COAST GUARD STATION

The Munising Coast Guard station at Sand Point, the present day headquarters building for the Pictured Rocks National Lakeshore, was built during the period 1932-33. It is typical of the small Coast Guard stations that dotted the Great Lakes during the first half of the twentieth century. Contrary to popular belief, the Munising station was never a United States Life-Saving Service station. That organization ceased to exist in 1915 when it was combined with the U.S. Revenue Marine to form the present day Coast Guard.

Specifications called for a "...two story frame dwelling, 30 feet by 45 feet, with concrete foundations; a one story frame boathouse, 37 feet by 55 feet, with creosote pile foundations; creosote wood pile and timber bulkheads, each 129 feet long; and a creosote timber and pile landing wharf, 10 by 40 feet."

The bid price for the construction was $12,230 by an Iron Mountain, Michigan contractor. The lookout tower and watch house were provided by the McClintic-Marshall Corporation of Bethlehem, Pennsylvania. It was one of eight built for the Coast Guard that year at a cost of $2,092 each. Erection on site added another $865 to the bill. The land for the station, some 7.1 acres, was acquired from the Cleveland Cliffs Iron Company for the nominal fee of $1.

It was hoped the station would be in operation on May 1, 1933, but thick ice in Munising Bay prevented the transfer of necessary boats and equipment from Marquette for more than two weeks. Finally at 8 a.m.

on May 16, the crew was formed up in front of the building; the activating orders read and Munising station officially placed in commission.

Throughout its operational life, the typical complement for the station included an officer-in-charge, bosun's mate first class, motor machinist's mate first class and seven surfmen.

Station equipment consisted of a 36-foot motor lifeboat, 26-foot motor surfboat, a small skiff and a cart-mounted beach apparatus. The latter was used when a vessel wrecked near shore. It consisted of a Lyle gun, a small cannon used to fire a messenger line from the beach to the ship, a faking box carrying the line and a breeches buoy together with heavier ropes, blocks and tackles. The breeches buoy was a ring buoy with a canvas seat attached used to transport sailors via an overhead line from ship to shore. All of the items were carried in the cart which could be pulled to the wreck site by the crew. The station also was allotted a new truck, but since the road to the station wasn't finished until 1934, its arrival was delayed until then.

Perhaps under the theory of giving them room to grow, the first inspection of the new station was not favorable. The commander of the Eleventh Coast Guard District complained that the floors were not neat enough, especially in the corners. Such inspections included not only the facility itself, but the men were required to demonstrate proficiency in "...boat drill, fire drill, wigwag, semaphore, flash-light, resuscitation," as well as in the manual of arms and marksmanship. When the crew demonstrated the required drills, he found that although they were proficient, "...the necessary snap is not seen at this station as at other stations." He further stated, "...the Officer-in-Charge seems to lack the knack of properly caring for and keeping up a station."

The station itself was far from finished. Much landscaping was needed, the lawn had to be planted and sidewalks constructed among a host of other tasks. The crew was expected to accomplish all of them, in addition to their regular duties. Once the road to Munising was finished, the station truck could be used to haul the necessary materials out from town.

Five months later, the crew had apparently jelled into a cohesive unit and a new inspection found major improvements, as the station received an excellent rating.

During the years prior to World War II, the station crew varied between 10 and 13 men. Daily routine consisted of various equipment drills and normal maintenance. Actual rescues were few. The men were called out to help small craft an average of twice a month. Usually it was nothing more than towing in a boat with a balky engine. During the winter they periodically put on snowshoes and went out on the ice to look for missing ice fishermen.

From August 14 to September 3, 1936, three crewmen were sent with the 36-foot motor lifeboat to Isle Royale to help fight a forest fire that eventually consumed 34,000 acres of timber. They joined crews and boats from Portage, Eagle Harbor, North Superior, Marquette and Grand Marais to carry fire fighters and supplies around the island. By mission's end, the Coast Guard crews had hauled 9,390 men and 242,000 pounds of supplies, covering a distance of 5,983 miles.

The station's role in the November 7, 1940 SPARTA rescue is described elsewhere. Their last major rescue occurred five days later when they received word via the Michigan Conservation Department that the steel steamer SINALOA was on the rocks at Sac Bay, near Fayette, Lake Michigan, about 80 miles south of Munising. Commercial fishermen had managed to remove 23 of her 42 man crew before the mountainous waves drove them off. The remaining 19 sailors were trapped aboard. Loading their gear aboard the station truck, they rattled off to the scene. There they discovered the only way to reach the beach opposite the wreck was through the woods, without a track of any kind to guide them. In a scene reminiscent of the HARTZELL rescue in October 1880 by the Point aux Bec Scies Life-Savers, the crew fought their way through the forest, pulling the rubber-tired cart by hand.

Arriving at 12:30 a.m., they found the big freighter lying broadside to the shore and about 500 feet out. They quickly went to work and within an hour and a half had a breeches buoy rigged and the first man ashore. Three hours later, all of the steamer's 19 remaining men were safe ashore. All seven members of the Munising crew that participated in the SINALOA rescue received the Commandant's Commendation for their efficient work.

Coast Guard crews are sometimes asked to do some strange things and the Munising crew was no different. When a bull moose was trapped on a ledge along the bluff at Miners Castle, the Michigan Conservation Department asked the crew to help drive it to safety. Rough seas prevented them from immediately approaching in their boat and when they returned two days later, the animal had disappeared, whether escaping on his own or drowning in the lake was never determined.

During World War II, the station complement increased dramatically, at one time reaching 28, as the Coast Guard sent new men for initial training before going on to operational units. When the war ended, manning decreased accordingly.

The inevitable change in technology spelled the end for many small Coast Guard stations, Munising among them. Better navigation equipment, including radar and radios, made commercial vessels safer and less prone to shipwreck. Helicopters, fixed wing aircraft and offshore cutters took over the search and rescue mission. Gone were the days of the 36-foot motor lifeboat driving off into the teeth of the gale on a desperate life or death mission. Like many lake stations, Munising also suffered from sand constantly filling in around the slip area, necessitating periodic dredging.

For a while the Munising station was manned by a skeleton crew of just a few men. Eventually with its abandonment in 1961, the land reverted to the Cleveland Cliffs Iron Company, who later deeded it to the city. In turn the city deeded it to the National Park Service for inclusion in the Pictured Rocks National Lakeshore.

GLOSSARY

Aft	Toward the stern.
Aground	Stranded in shallow water.
Amidships	Midway between bow and stern.
Arch	A curved reinforcing structure of wood or iron running the length of a ship.
Ashore	Stranded on or near the shore.
Bar	A shoal of sand or gravel.
Bark	A 3- to 5-masted sailing vessel with only the foremast square rigged, the others being fore-and-aft rigged
Bateau	(plural Bateaux) French for boat, refers to a light, flat-bottomed boat, usually rigged with a single square sail.
Beam	The width of a vessel.
Beam ends	"On beam ends" means listing so far as to nearly capsize.
Bilge	The lowest level inside a vessel.
Bilge pump	Pump used to remove water from the bilge.
Bloom	A bar of iron from a forge.
Bobstay	A rope or chain used to steady the bowsprit.
Boom	1. A spar extending from a mast to hold the foot of a sail.
	2. A barrier composed of a chain of floating logs enclosing other free-floating logs.

Bow	The front end of a vessel.
Bowsprit	A spar extending from the bow of a ship.
Brig	A two-masted vessel with both masts square rigged.
Bulk freighter	A power vessel designed to carry cargos such as ore, stone, coal or grain.
Bulkhead	A wall or partition aboard a vessel.
Bulwark	The part of a ship's side which is above the deck.
Cabin trunk	An opening in which a cabin is recessed into a deck.
Capsize	To overturn.
Capstan	A drum-like device usually standing on the foredeck and used for heaving in anchors, hoisting sails and other heavy work.
Centerboard	A flat board which can be lowered below the bottom of a sailing vessel to reduce lateral travel.
Centerboard trunk	The box into which a centerboard is retracted.
Chainplate	A metal strap used to anchor the shrouds to the side of the hull.
Coke	Coal from which all volatile material has been driven off.
Consort	A vessel frequently towed by another; usually seen in a steamer and schooner-barge relationship.
Coston signal	A bright colored flare used for signalling.
Crosshead	An iron cap at the top of a rudder stock with slotted arms to engage the steering gear.
Davit	A small crane used to raise and lower a ship's boat.
Deadwood	Reinforcing between the keelson and the stem or sternpost.
Deck	The "floor" of a boat.
Deck load	Cargo carried on deck rather than in a hold.
Depth	The depth of a vessel's hold (rather than the depth of water needed to float the vessel.)

Drydock	A basin from which the water can be drained so that a vessel can be repaired below the waterline.
Faking box	A box in which a shot line is coiled to avoid tangling when it is payed out.
Fiferail	A rail around the mast where rigging is secured with belaying pins.
Flotsam	Wreckage left floating after a vessel sinks.
Fo'c's'le	Forecastle.
Fore	At or toward the bow.
Forecastle	A cabin in the bow of a vessel, commonly below deck, usually the crew's quarters.
Foredeck	The forward part of the main deck.
Foremast	The forwardmost mast.
Foresail	The large sail on the foremast.
Founder	To sink.
Frame	One of the transverse structural members of a ship.
Gaff	A spar extending from a mast to hold the head of a sail.
Gale	A very strong wind, officially 32 to 63 miles per hour.
Galley	A ship's kitchen.
Gangway	An opening in a vessel's side through which freight or passengers may be taken aboard.
Hamper	Usually used in reference to the rigging used for upper spars, as in "top-hamper."
Hard hat diver	A diver using surface-supplied diving gear including a metal helmet.
Hatch	An opening in the deck of a vessel leading to a hold.
Hawser	A rope or cable used for towing.
Hold	The interior of a ship below decks where cargo is stowed.
Hogging arch	A curved reinforcing structure built into the planking of a vessel.

Hulett unloader	A large clamshell bucket used to unload iron ore from a freighter's hold.
Hull	The main body of a ship.
Hurricane deck	The upper deck of a passenger steamer.
Jettison	To throw overboard.
Jib	A triangular sail set between the foremast and the jib boom.
Jib boom	A spar forming a continuation of the bowsprit.
Jibe	To shift a fore-and-aft sail from one side of a vessel to the other; during this maneuver the boom swings rapidly across the deck.
Keel	The backbone of a ship, a strong member running from bow to stern on the bottom of the vessel.
Keelson	A reinforcement for the keel inside the hull.
Laker	1. A Great lakes bulk freighter.
	2. One of a series of cargo ships built on the Great Lakes during World War I.
Lifeboat	1. A boat carried aboard ship to allow persons aboard to abandon ship in case of shipwreck.
	2. A large rescue craft, either oar- or engine-powered.
Light	1. A lighthouse.
	2. Without cargo.
Lighter	1. A barge used to unload cargo from a vessel.
	2. To unload with lighters.
Lock	A section of a canal in which a vessel is raised or lowered by changing the water level.
Lumber hooker	A steamer designed to haul lumber.
Lyle gun	A small cannon used to throw a rescue line to a vessel in distress.

Mackinaw boat	A small sailing vessel, usually fore-and-aft rigged with a large mainmast and a smaller mizzenmast.
Mainmast	The taller mast of a two-masted vessel, or the second mast on a vessel with three or more masts.
Mainsail	The large sail on the mainmast.
Mizzen	The large fore-and-aft sail on the mizzenmast.
Mizzenmast	The mast immediately aft of the mainmast.
Northwester	A storm from the northwest, common on the Great Lakes; also referred to as a "nor'wester."
Package freighter	A freighter designed to carry freight in boxes, barrels, etc.
Pig	A bar of iron from a blast furnace.
Pilothouse	An enclosed area from which a vessel is controlled.
Port	The left side of a ship.
Portlight	A porthole, including its frame, glass and cover.
Promenade deck	The deck below the hurricane deck.
Propeller	A steam vessel driven by a propeller.
Quadrant	A quarter-circular fitting used to turn a rudder.
Quarter	The section of a vessel's side just ahead of the stern.
Raft	A quantity of logs towed inside a boom.
Reef	A ridge of rock which comes near the surface of a lake.
Rigging	The various ropes, chains and cables which support and operate the masts and sails of a vessel.
Schooner	A fore-and-aft rigged vessel with two or more masts. Other types of sailing vessels often were generically referred to as "schooners" on the Lakes.
Schooner-barge	A schooner which has had its topmasts removed and carries only minimal sail, commonly towed behind a steamer or tug.

Scow	A large flat-bottomed boat with blunt ends used for rough cargo or as a lighter.
Scow schooner	A cheaply-built sailing vessel with a flat bottom, flat sides and a square bow and stern, generally used for cargo of low value.
Shroud	A rope or cable used to brace a mast from side to side.
Sidewheeler	A steam vessel with paddle wheels on either side of the hull.
Sloop	A fore-and-aft rigged sailboat with one mast.
Soo	Sault Ste. Marie
Spar	A long, rounded timber used as a mast, boom, gaff, etc.
Specie	Hard currency; coins.
Squall	A brief, sudden windstorm.
Stanchion	A vertical support for a rail or deck beam.
Starboard	The right side of a ship.
Stay	A rope or cable used to brace a mast fore and aft.
Staysail	A triangular sail set on a stay aft of the jib.
Steam barge	A wooden propeller-driven steamship built for carrying freight.
Steamer	A steam-powered vessel.
Stem	The main vertical timber at the bow of a ship.
Step	To install or position a mast.
Stern	The rear end of a vessel.
Sternpost	The main vertical timber at the stern of a ship.
Stock	1. The crossbar on an anchor.
	2. The vertical extension of a rudder by which it is turned.
Surfboat	A small rowing boat, usually 24-26-foot in length, typically used by the men of the U.S. Life-Saving Service for rescues of distressed sailors.
Tiller	An arm used to turn a rudder.

Ton	Nautically speaking, 100 cubic feet of cargo capacity.
Topmast	The upper part of a two-part mast.
Topsail	The second sail above the deck on any mast.
Topsail schooner	A schooner which carries a square topsail on the fore top-mast.
Tow barge	A vessel built or converted to be towed behind another vessel.
Trunk cabin	A cabin which is recessed partly below deck level.
Voyageur	A boatman employed by fur companies to transport furs.
Watch	Duty period aboard ship, normally four hours in duration.
Whaleback	A Great Lakes steam-powered bulk freighter with a distinctive rounded steel hull.
Wheel	1. A ship's steering wheel or helm.
	2. A ship's propeller.
	3. A paddle wheel
Winch	A hoisting machine with a horizontal drum for raising sails, centerboard, etc.
Windlass	A large hoisting machine with a horizontal drum for raising the anchor, etc.
Wrecker	One who recovers or salvages wrecked vessels.
Yawl	1. A ship's small boat, propelled by oars.
	2. A two-masted fore-and-aft rigged vessel with a small mast stepped aft of the rudder.

INDEX

ABOUT THE AUTHORS

FREDERICK STONEHOUSE holds a Master of Arts Degree in History from Northern Michigan University, Marquette, Michigan, and has authored six books on Great Lakes Vessel losses. *Isle Royale Shipwrecks, Went Missing, Munising Shipwrecks, Lake Superior's "Shipwreck Coast," Keweenaw Shipwrecks* and *The Wreck of the Edmund Fitzgerald* are all published by Avery Color Studios.

He has also been a consultant for both the U.S. National Park Service and Parks Canada.

His articles have been published in *Skin Diver, Great Lakes Cruiser Magazine* and *Diver* Magazines. He has been a member of the Great Lakes Historical and Marquette County Historical Societies, the Lake Superior Marine Museum Association, the Alger Underwater Preserve Committee, a member of the Board of Directors of the Marquette Maritime Museum and a member of the Board of Directors of the United States Life-Saving Service Heritage Association.

DANIEL R. FOUNTAIN has been researching, diving, and exploring shipwrecks for over 17 years. Raised in the Upper Peninsula of Michigan, Dan has always been attracted by the lure of the Great Lakes. He spends much of his time researching historical records, searching for shipwrecks, diving, and documenting the wrecks and the stories of the gallant people who make up the Great Lakes' rich history.

Dan holds an Associate Degree in Electronics from Northern Michigan University. He has previously authored a comprehensive book on the history of gold mining in Michigan's Upper Peninsula. In addition to research and diving, Dan enjoys prospecting, cross-country skiing, and traveling. Dan and his wife, Judy, reside in Negaunee, Michigan.